Building a Prototype Church

Book 1 of the Prototype Church Series

The Church is in a Season of Profound of Change

Bill Vincent

Building a Prototype Church

© 2016 by Bill Vincent.

All rights reserved. No part of this book may be reproduced, stored in a retrieval system or transmitted in any form or by any means without the prior written permission of the publishers, except by a reviewer who may quote brief passages in a review to be printed in a newspaper, magazine or journal.

Softcover 978-1-365-82357-2

PUBLISHED BY REVIVAL WAVES OF GLORY BOOKS & PUBLISHING

www.revivalwavesofgloryministries.com

Litchfield, IL

Published in the United States of America

Table of Contents

CHAPTER ONE Building a Prototype Church 4
CHAPTER TWO Change Your Mind-set 13
CHAPTER THREE Character and Honor 25
CHAPTER FOUR The New Church 28
CHAPTER FIVE The Inner Channel 34
CHAPTER SIX What Are We Giving Birth To? 36
CHAPTER SEVEN Who Are the Helpers of God? 39
CHAPTER EIGHT Dreams & Interpretation of Dreams 48
CHAPTER NINE God Is Doing a New Thing 64
CHAPTER TEN Does God Share Your Theology? 73
CHAPTER ELEVEN Paradigm Shift 82
CHAPTER TWELVE Servant Leaders 87
CHAPTER THIRTEEN Dunamis Power 91
CHAPTER FOURTEEN God's Will For Healing 95
CHAPTER FIFTEEN Building the Kingdom 100
CHAPTER SIXTEEN Fasting Transforms Lives 108
CHAPTER SEVENTEEN Misusing the Prophetic Gift 120
CHAPTER EIGHTEEN Obedience – Not Sacrifice 124
CHAPTER NINETEEN Ministry Women Come Forth 134
CHAPTER TWENTY The Transforming Fire of God's Power 147
CHAPTER TWENTY ONE Christ Centered Prototype Church 167
CHAPTER TWENTY TWO The Anointed Eagles 173
CHAPTER TWENTY THREE The Fire of God In Power 178
CHAPTER TWENTY FOUR The Kingly Anointing 186
CHAPTER TWENTY FIVE The Kingdom Mandate 192
CHAPTER TWENTY SIX Spiritual Dynamics 199
About the Author 204
Recommended Books 205

Chapter One
Building a Prototype Church

For the last few hundred years the Church has been spinning out of control. Where the Church stands today is no real match for the Early Church. This book is being released for the purpose of restoring the Church and also raising up a new type of Church called a Prototype.

Things rarely happen quite the way we imagine they should. No matter how hard we plan and strategize, keep the chain of command small to avoid confusion, work through tightly defined parameters, and generally/specifically keep on top of things, it doesn't seem to matter. I am here to tell you this book is directed by the Holy Spirit and is sure to stir some religion up.

Some odd variable that we had not anticipated will creep into the mix somewhere and upset everything.

Imagine that you are at the hub of full-blown revival. There has been a powerful move of God that has torn down all your cozy ideas and practices about church.

The wind of the Spirit has filled you and your church with a compelling need to evangelize and go up against demonic forces everywhere you find them.

Even the weaker brethren are now to a far higher level of anointing than your strongest preachers had *before* the move of God began! Thousands are being saved. Sick bodies are healed; demons are cast out; and the nation is being turned upside down.

The Church is in a Season of Profound of Change

Are you ready for this type of Church? I'm here to tell you this is your day to take hold of the plans God has for today.

The body of believers not caught up in this new move are against it, criticizing it as dangerous phenomena and preaching dire warnings about control, manipulation, and mental ill health. Any one whom is a critic is criticizing the Holy Spirit in this move. It is easy to speak against something you don't fully understand. Listen you need to be open to what God wants to do.

The government is stirred up by the whole commotion, and there are various investigations underway or planned against this supposed new cultic activity.

You have never seen such a level of power, grace, and holiness of God all at one time. The church is outgrowing itself month by month.

Are you ready for miracles as commonplace; the amazing and incredible presence of God to be everywhere. The team that you are part of, which is caught up in the epicenter of all this activity, is the most profound experience that you have ever encountered. Of course, there are problems—problems that often are huge and time-consuming. However, as you pray for wisdom, the anointing to move forward is so great that godly insight seems to spring into your conscious mind with ease.

During the moving forward to becoming a prototype Church you will find oppositions. Every day brings a pressure cocktail of more people, more needs, greater opposition, further demonic attacks, fresh misunderstandings, calculated misinterpretations, added responsibilities, supplementary clerical problems to overcome, and extra requirements for advice, leadership, and ministry. Everything is strained to the limit of personal and physical ability. One thing that will surely cause a quicker finished Church is Revival. Revival seems to be concerned with endurance and stamina as much as it is preoccupied with anointing and empowerment. You are in the midst of constant attack and blessing; of tiredness, pressure, and opposition; of trying to keep everything going smoothly so that more people can be touched and reached; of not losing people to poor organization and mismanagement.

You do not want this move to blow through society, touching thousands of lives, but not see church built at the end of it. Indeed, it shows no signs of tapering off! Are you getting excited about a new move of God?

The need to develop leaders and train people to look after others, the need for more prayer, and the demand for more workers is huge. You are caught up in the whole wonderful and demanding, exhausting mix of a move of God. The implications and repercussions are going to hit everyone, hard. You don't need this pressure right now.

All your prayers have been focused on asking the Lord for wisdom and strength to keep this ship steady so that the work of harvesting souls can continue unhindered.

Other members of your core team are up in arms about this new move. Not only is this an additional pressure that will give your enemies greater ammunition against you, but you also are losing some key people who want to be a part of this new thing.

Rumors increase—angels, visions, trances, visitations, audible voices of God. The new move has become a focal point for dealing with people of other religions whose leaders are now up in arms, shouting about holy wars, and religious persecution. This is all in God's Plan to expose hearts of the religious goats that seem to rise up as God's Glory rises.

The uproar around the work increases enormously. Surely this is not right? How can this be God? Why, when there are apostles, prophets, and other fivefold ministries working in team, when thousands of people are praying daily for wisdom and grace, when the power of God is being demonstrated daily on every street corner? We ask God to move and when He does it causes us to fear it's not Him.

The Church is in a Season of Profound of Change

Why start a new move of God, a new revival, when the current one is turning the world upside down? Why choose this particular brother who is hardly noted for his calm, common sense rationale?

Incredibly, we now have three things happening on a major level within the world of the people of God. Firstly, the word of faith and hope is passed down successfully from one Godly generation to another—the foundation of all spiritual experience. Secondly, this "new" move of the Spirit is causing outrageous problems for the religious establishment of the day—not to mention the secular government. Thirdly, this upstart, outrageous, and frankly idiotic new thing is stirring up all the rest of the people that the first new movement of God (revival) was not concerned with. Are you confused?

I am really trying to lay a big foundation for this book. It is only now that many are really COMING INTO ALL OF THIS. I can only imagine the uproar if it actually happened. Of course, we know that it did happen. In Acts 10 is the biblical account of a move of God beginning with God sending an angel to a non-Christian? God then chose the most impulsive, reckless, and radical believer—Peter—to instigate a new move before the current one was even firing on all cylinders.

Trances, repeated visions, audible voices of God, angelic visitation, unclean contact with other religions and fake gods, probable demonic manifestations and the Holy Spirit falling on people before the message was concluded, an appeal given and response for salvation—all had occurred! This is not God! Is it?

If we really look at the life of Jesus on the earth we will find He would not be received today as a man of God. We a Church don't receive God manifested when He is right in front of us.

Is it small wonder that those back in Jerusalem were demanding an explanation? I wonder how many seminary rules were broken by God and Peter. What possible theological thinking could be used to justify these insane events? What Scriptures would be quoted? Surely his explanation had to be founded on something more than just subjective experience: "I was in a trance; I saw a vision; I heard a voice; I went where the voice told me; I was in the house of an occult guy who had seen an angel; this angel told him about me (I don't know why me and not you guys!). While I was explaining the gospel, the Holy Spirit fell on them like He had with us"

Acts 11:4-15 But Peter rehearsed *the matter* from the beginning, and expounded *it* by order unto them, saying, I was in the city of Joppa praying: and in a trance I saw a vision, A certain vessel descend, as it had been a great sheet, let down from heaven by four corners; and it came even to me: Upon the which when I had fastened mine eyes, I considered, and saw fourfooted beasts of the earth, and wild beasts, and creeping things, and fowls of the air. And I heard a voice saying unto me, Arise, Peter; slay and eat. But I said, Not so, Lord: for nothing common or unclean hath at any time entered into my mouth. But the voice answered me again from heaven, What God hath cleansed, *that* call not thou common. And this was done three times: and all were drawn up again into heaven. And, behold, immediately there were three men already come unto the house where I was, sent from Caesarea unto me. And the Spirit bade me go with them, nothing doubting. Moreover these six brethren accompanied me, and we entered into the man's house: And he shewed us how he had seen an angel in his house, which stood and said unto him, Send men to Joppa, and call for Simon, whose surname is Peter; Who shall tell thee words, whereby thou and all thy house shall be saved. And as I began to speak, the Holy Ghost fell on them, as on us at the beginning.

Peter completes his explanation with these incredible words:

Acts 11:17 Forasmuch then as God gave them the like gift as *he did* unto us, who believed on the Lord Jesus Christ; what was I, that I could withstand God?

Unbelievable, but scriptural!

The early Church was in full flow of anointing and power—thousands entering the Kingdom of God; apostles and prophets interacting; evangelists being transported through time and space to keep divine appointments to bring salvation; teachers instructing new converts; pastors putting together systems of care and culture. The supernatural was natural and it so shall be today. The sick were being laid out in the streets, and society was excited with all the events of revival. No one dared to join the church with its radical expression of Kingdom life; however, thousands were being added.

Acts 2:41-47 Then they that gladly received his word were baptized: and the same day there were added *unto them* about three thousand souls. And they continued stedfastly in the apostles' doctrine and fellowship, and in breaking of bread, and in prayers. And fear came upon every soul: and many wonders and signs were done by the apostles. And all that believed were together, and had all things common; And sold their possessions and goods, and parted them to all *men,* as every man had need. And they, continuing daily with one accord in the temple, and breaking bread from house to house, did eat their meat with gladness and singleness of heart, Praising God, and having favour with all the people. And the Lord added to the church daily such as should be saved.

Acts 4:32-37 And the multitude of them that believed were of one heart and of one soul: neither said any *of them* that ought of the things which he possessed was his own; but they had all things common. And with great power gave the apostles witness of the resurrection of the Lord Jesus: and great grace was upon them all. Neither was there any among them that lacked: for as many as were possessors of lands or houses sold them, and brought the prices of the things that were sold, And laid *them* down at the apostles' feet: and distribution was made unto every man according as he had need. And Joses, who by the apostles was surnamed Barnabas, (which is, being interpreted, The son of consolation,) a Levite, *and* of the country of Cyprus, Having land, sold *it,* and brought the money, and laid *it* at the apostles' feet.

Acts 5:12-16 And by the hands of the apostles were many signs and wonders wrought among the people; (and they were all with one accord in Solomon's porch. And of the rest durst no man join himself to them: but the people magnified them. And believers were the more added to the Lord, multitudes both of men and women.) Insomuch that they brought forth the sick into the streets, and laid *them* on beds and couches, that at the least the shadow of Peter passing by might overshadow some of them. There came also a multitude *out* of the cities round about unto Jerusalem, bringing sick folks, and them which were vexed with unclean spirits: and they were healed every one.

This is the stuff of dreams for the modern-day Church, representing the full range of all we are praying for and longing to see. It has been what all real intercessors have cried out for. If we could have these same problems! With all this phenomenal activity in the early Church, is it not strange that God wants to do a new work but cannot break into the existing structure of church?

We can perhaps better understand the dilemma in this modern time. The early Church was steeped in the culture and passion of revival. Why did they not receive internal direction in their apostolic prayer meetings? For some reason, the Lord could not break into the hearts and minds of the people He was using the most. A mind-set is a mind-set is a mind-set, even if it is surrounded by incredible events and extraordinary spiritual dynamics. It doesn't matter if we say we agree with this new found prototype we must change our actions to truly agree. We would suppose that they would be wide open to every tone of what the Lord was saying. There is a lesson for us here. No matter how good we are at hearing the Lord, how excellent at obedience and faith, how in tune with the things of God, there is always something more in the movement of the Holy Spirit than we are currently experiencing. It would seem that no matter how wide open we think we are to the things of God; layers of prejudice, hidden mind-sets, and current practices can be broken only by God's touch.

Understand that our nature of the flesh is in the way. It is not in our nature to perceive new things while still being jolted by recent events. We do become self-satisfied with blessings, so easily preoccupied by all that is happening—a lot of it no doubt good and incredible.

Sometimes the biggest threat to a new move is not the old one that is not working, but the move that is still working and doing well. We can never be satisfied of the place we attain. The current cutting edge movement will be obsolete in the next season. Never stay at one level but press in to the next and the next and the next.

Somehow I don't believe we will have a traditional revival, sweeping wave that will hit a country and take everything with it. I don't think it will be an outpouring centered on key, international, and high-profile ministries. I think it will be a people revival. I feel that God will use a nameless, faceless generation of people, unknown in the earth. It will be a Gideon's revival, led by the least among us who have been powerfully touched.

Think about it! Will God use the high priest, church councils, and key ministries, or pick up a bunch of illiterate fishermen and sprinkle them with a mixture of different personalities with educated upbringings of varying types?

It will be different. He will come to people with open minds and hearts, people who do not set things in concrete practice.

He will come to people who understand that with all that God has given us, with all He has graciously blessed us, we need to be mindful that there are new things God will want to do—which may not fit with what He has already given us.

This "revival" may not be just one type. God only builds prototypes, the first in a series. We build stereotypes, many of the exact same type! We build stereotypes because we are not creative enough. The Lord does not build stereotypes because He is too creative.

There needs to be hundreds and thousands of different types of church in order for the Body of Christ to accurately reflect the vastness of Heaven and the creativity of God. We reproduce our own kind. If we are dead we produce dead.

In character, God is the Father of conformity. Everyone must be like Jesus. In creativity, He is the Father of diversity, expressing Himself as fully in the Church as He has in creation.

I think we will have dozens of revivals, each one specific in its application and operation; each aimed at differing elements in society, at varying people-groups. You will be able to see more about this in my next book "Glory: Revival Presence of God".

God is generationally inclined. "I am the God of Abraham, Isaac, and Jacob." There may be a children's revival, a young people's movement, and a move of the Spirit upon the elderly to release the Caleb anointing. It may be among families, the educated, the poor, prisoners, business people, the arts community, politicians, lawyers, even church people themselves!

In the midst of revival, God has to send an angel to a devout man of a different religion because His own people are too preoccupied with what they are doing—or their mind-set is too narrow—to hear what God wants to do next. The Church has been so closed minded for generations. The faith is a weak version compared to the Apostles in the New Testament. Every time I move into a new thing some Church leader tries to convince people I'm of a wrong spirit. I'm talking about when miracles, signs and wonders come, when people break out in laughter and fall all over the place they try to disprove.

CHAPTER TWO
Change Your Mind-set

We have to have our old ways replaced by the new moves of God. By far, the greatest hindrance to a new move of God is the way we think about the old one. All his life Peter had been brought up in a particular way.

Although acknowledging the presence of God in his reply, Peter feels safe in his tradition to obstruct the cause of God and disobey the Lord's command.

Acts 10:14 But Peter said, **Not so, Lord; for I have never eaten any thing that is common or unclean.**

Tradition is bigger than God when we put it first.

Without a change of mind, Peter cannot move into the fresh anointing and new ministry that God is releasing. I previously stated that each new visitation is accompanied by a revelation of God's principles and a testing of His purposes. Many leaders are wanting all the new until it doesn't look like the old.

Each thing that God does, involves a test of our submission and commitment to Him. Can Peter be trusted with the new move of God? The answer lies in his ability to cast off a mind-set that has long governed his life.

It is like God to strike at the very heart of our past experience in order to release us into a new move of the Spirit. I'm talking, of a basic practice that was a significant part of Peter's experience and tradition.

A change of mind was demanded as a prerequisite to participating in a major new move of God.

Peter was horrified: "Not so, Lord!" He did not understand that he was in a new day, a new era of the Spirit. He had heard Jesus say on numerous occasions, "You have heard it said...now I say to you," thus signifying major alterations to perception and practice. It had not computed though into any determined areas of change. Peter had one way of thinking until God demanded a change of mind-set: "Do not consider things this way any longer" was the Lord's response to Peter's mind-set.

When the Lord does a new thing, He releases a new mind to His people so that they can submit and be involved. A new dimension involves a new mind-set. You need to take hold of this.

The work of renewal in recent years did not compute with many churches. Instead of allowing the Lord to fulfill His purpose, they chose rationale, putting Scripture in line with their own mind-set to justify their non-involvement. "Renewal does not fit in with what God is doing with us," they observed. Actually, it was their mind-set that probably did not suit the purpose of God.

It was easier to point to phenomena as a way of justifying their behavior. The Holy Spirit may well have a different perspective, as we will discover as each one's work and life receive judgment, either in this life or the one to come. It has been my own experience that many judge from the unknown such as the supernatural realm.

Zacharias could not change his mind-set when presented with an angelic visitation and prophetic word about a new son

Luke 1:5-20 There was in the days of Herod, the king of Judaea, a certain priest named Zacharias, of the course of Abia: and his wife *was* of the daughters of Aaron, and her name *was* Elisabeth. And they were both righteous before God, walking in all the commandments and ordinances of the Lord blameless. And they had no child, because that Elisabeth was barren, and they both were *now* well stricken in years. And it came to pass, that while he executed the priest's office before God in the order of his course,

According to the custom of the priest's office, his lot was to burn incense when he went into the temple of the Lord. And the whole multitude of the people were praying without at the time of incense. And there appeared unto him an angel of the Lord standing on the right side of the altar of incense. And when Zacharias saw *him*, he was troubled, and fear fell upon him. But the angel said unto him, Fear not, Zacharias: for thy prayer is heard; and thy wife Elisabeth shall bear thee a son, and thou shalt call his name John. And thou shalt have joy and gladness; and many shall rejoice at his birth. For he shall be great in the sight of the Lord, and shall drink neither wine nor strong drink; and he shall be filled with the Holy Ghost, even from his mother's womb. And many of the children of Israel shall he turn to the Lord their God. And he shall go before him in the spirit and power of Elias, to turn the hearts of the fathers to the children, and the disobedient to the wisdom of the just; to make ready a people prepared for the Lord. And Zacharias said unto the angel, Whereby shall I know this? for I am an old man, and my wife well stricken in years. And the angel answering said unto him, I am Gabriel, that stand in the presence of God; and am sent to speak unto thee, and to shew thee these glad tidings. And, behold, thou shalt be dumb, and not able to speak, until the day that these things shall be performed, because thou believest not my words, which shall be fulfilled in their season.

He was struck silent as a result of his mental and spiritual disobedience and unbelief. "How shall I know this?" is an extremely arrogant question when faced with a heavenly being one that is representing Almighty God.

Whenever intellect is raised above spiritual response, it always puts us on the wrong side of God. I've seen it in my own life before my eyes were open to the supernatural realm.

Man who have elevated intellectual Christianity above experience, whereas charismatics have kissed their brains good-bye in the pursuit of spiritual encounter. Both mind-sets have to conform to the Lord in humble obedience. We have to find the balance and keep the Word of God as our guide at all times. Mary's response, in an experience similar to that of Zacharias', seemed to be similar as well.

Luke 1:34 Then said Mary unto the angel, **How shall this be, seeing I know not a man?**

However, in reality, it was very different. Zacharias' underlying question really was, "How do I know you are telling the truth?" He questioned the integrity of the messenger who was rightly insulted and made this response:

Luke 1:19 **And the angel answering said unto him, I am Gabriel, that stand in the presence of God**; and am sent to speak unto thee, and to shew thee these glad tidings.

To question his integrity was to criticize the Lord; therefore, a punishment was required to teach a lesson. Mary's response was quite different. She was not questioning *if* it would occur, but *how* it would happen. Her attitude seemed to be, "Great. How will it happen, since I do not know a man?" The angel gave her an appropriate answer, to which Mary's response was,

Luke 1:34-38 Then said Mary unto the angel, **How shall this be, seeing I know not a man?** And the angel answered and said unto her, **The Holy Ghost shall come upon thee**, and the power of the Highest shall overshadow thee: therefore also that holy thing which shall be born of thee shall be called the Son of God. And, behold, thy cousin Elisabeth, she hath also conceived a son in her old age: and this is the sixth month with her, who was called barren. For with God nothing shall be impossible. And Mary said, Behold the handmaid of the Lord; be it unto me according to thy word. And the angel departed from her.

The issue is, we must be prepared to let go of old mind-sets and be influenced by God's thinking so that we enter into new paradigms of His calling and purpose. Change is coming but the thing is we have to change with it.

Spiritual change begins with a renewal of mind.

Romans 12:2 And be not conformed to this world: but be ye transformed by the renewing of your mind, that ye may prove what *is* that good, and acceptable, and perfect, will of God.

In order to prove the current will of God, we may need a release from our understanding of His previous will. In the past, His will may have been for meetings and mission to be conducted in a particular way. However, His will at this time may call for a fresh strategy and method. Unless our mind is changed, the new knowledge of His will remains unknown or unappreciated. We become ineffective and irrelevant. Transformation in reality always begins in the mind. To walk closely with God, we must win the battle for the mind.

1Corinthians 2:9-16 But as it is written, Eye hath not seen, nor ear heard, neither have entered into the heart of man, the things which God hath prepared for them that love him. But God hath revealed *them* unto us by his Spirit: for the Spirit searcheth all things, yea, the deep things of God. For what man knoweth the things of a man, save the spirit of man which is in him? even so the things of God knoweth no man, but the Spirit of God. Now we have received, not the spirit of the world, but the spirit which is of God; that we might know the things that are freely given to us of God. Which things also we speak, not in the words which man's wisdom teacheth, but which the Holy Ghost teacheth; comparing spiritual things with spiritual. But the natural man receiveth not the things of the Spirit of God: for they are foolishness unto him: neither can he know *them,* because they are spiritually discerned. But he that is spiritual judgeth all things, yet he himself is judged of no man. For who hath known the mind of the Lord, that he may instruct him? But we have the mind of Christ.

The close connection between mind, God, and heart must be recovered fully—not just the ability to understand the revealed truth of Scripture, but actually the capacity to know the mind of God in terms of our life. The Lord has thoughts about us daily. He knows what He wants to say to us; what our response should be; what and how He wants us to pray; what we should contemplate in study of the Word; what we must meditate on to expands our revelation of

Him. He knows who He wants us to meet and the direction our life should take over a period of time. (What we call guidance, He calls relationship.) His plans for next year probably began last year or before. He thinks long-term. When you go to a meeting where you are stretched beyond where you have been, God is directing a new thing. A seemingly insignificant meeting with someone today may have great repercussions in several years' time.

Life is perceived in the Spirit first before it can be understood in the mind. In the Acts 10 account, we read that Peter was greatly perplexed in mind as to what everything meant.

Acts 10:17 Now while Peter doubted in himself what this vision which he had seen should mean, behold, the men which were sent from Cornelius had made enquiry for Simon's house, and stood before the gate,

There was a great struggle going on in his head, which he was losing. The Lord had to tell him to go "doubting nothing"

Acts 10:20 Arise therefore, and get thee down, and go with them, doubting nothing: for I have sent them.

Peter still asked the men for the reason they had come because the battle in his thought life was still raging.

Acts 10:21 Then Peter went down to the men which were sent unto him from Cornelius; and said, Behold, I am he whom ye seek: what *is* the cause wherefore ye are come?

He went out of pure obedience but still asked the same question several days later in Joppa.

Acts 10:29 Therefore came I *unto you* without gainsaying, as soon as I was sent for: I ask therefore for what intent ye have sent for me?

Suddenly, as Cornelius was speaking, something clicked in Peter's spirit and he said,

Acts 10:34 Then Peter opened *his* mouth, and said, **Of a truth I perceive that God is no respecter of persons:**

We need the mind of the Lord to understand what God has said and done in times past; to understand what God is saying and doing in times present; and to know what God is saying now about what He will do in time to come. What we are most comfortable with is very well the thing that is keeping you from the things to come.

There is a quality of spiritual perception that we receive in our heart relationship with God that unlocks our natural mind and causes us to think on a different wavelength.

The thoughts and the ways of God are altogether different from ours. We have received the Spirit of God so that we may know about everything that God wants to give to us.

Isaiah 55:8, 9 For my thoughts *are* not your thoughts, neither *are* your ways my ways, saith the LORD. For *as* the heavens are higher than the earth, so are my ways higher than your ways, and my thoughts than your thoughts.

We are taught to think like God by the Spirit. He combines spiritual thoughts with spiritual words, revealing the mind of the Lord. The more we understand the mind of God, the quicker our maturity develops into experience and anticipation in Him. When we understand that the Lord is principle-centered and therefore unchanging, we relax greatly in our knowing of Him. We wait for Him patiently and willingly because we know He will come. We are no longer worried because we have learned in our mind and heart that when God gives us a promise, His word is just as good as the action of it.

Some of the wisdom and ways of God are difficult to comprehend at first. Generally, that is because we make our mind the critical point of reception and the focal point of belief. We have been brought up as Christians in a way to receive only what we can see not what is unseen. This has made us critical to think God will show us Himself in His fullness. The mind is an instrument; it is the heart that receives acknowledgment. Your heart receives revelation; your mind receives information. Your mind applies what your heart admits.

Proverbs 3:5, 6 Trust in the LORD with all thine heart; and lean not unto thine own understanding. In all thy ways acknowledge him, and he shall direct thy paths.

Our mind and Spirit has to be in unity in everything. There is a divine order created for your mind to find peace and rest before the Lord. The heart is for trusting and acknowledging; the mind is for understanding and guidance. The combination of both together, in the right order, will keep us moving on freely in the purposes and will of God. We have the mind of the Lord as we have His heart.

We love and trust God in all things. We express that trust in worship, praise, and lack of anxiety. The more we acknowledge Him and express our trust, the more the burden of worry is replaced by a depth of peace and rest. This is important, because it is through rest that revelation moves from heart to mind. God will change your mind all the time on how you do things.

Worry closes our mind to faith and peace. We cannot experience God when our mind is in confusion. Worship releases divine order. A heart full of trust and rest creates a mind of peace. Then faith is the vehicle that takes revelation out of our heart and into our conscious mind. Meditation is the combination of heart and mind working together to expand our conscious understanding of the Lord. It will release not only knowledge, but also a capacity to experience that knowledge now. When you're at home play worship music even if it is low and it will change your atmosphere.

Revelation and information produce transformation. The mind is renewed by its submission to the heart. It is not just revelatory facts that the mind picks up from the heart. It is the Spirit of revelation itself. The Spirit that releases revelation to the heart is passed on to the mind—spiritual thoughts combining through spiritual words. It is the mind of Christ, who always acknowledged from His heart the words and works of His Father. It is a cycle that occurs continuously at different speeds. Some cycles are annual, monthly, weekly, or even daily. You can receive the cycle from God or the devil. But with the cycle of God allow it all to come from the Spirit through the thoughts. A cycle begins and ends in God. Scripture links God's thoughts and ways with nature:

Isaiah 55:8-11 For my thoughts *are* not your thoughts, neither *are* your ways my ways, saith the LORD. For *as* the heavens are higher than the earth, so are my ways higher than your ways, and my thoughts than your thoughts. For as the rain cometh down, and the snow from heaven, and returneth not thither, but watereth the earth, and maketh it bring forth and bud, that it may give seed to the sower, and bread to the eater: So shall my word be that goeth forth out of my mouth: it shall not return unto me void, but it shall accomplish that which I please, and it shall prosper *in the thing* whereto I sent it.

Water from heaven produces growth in the earth before returning to God. He is Alpha and Omega. Everything begins in Him and ends with Him. Even His love is a cycle. We love Him because He first loved us and His love affected our life profoundly. Even revelation flows from God to our trusting heart, which is deeply affected. The heart combines with the mind, bringing renewal of thought and transformation of life. Transformation of life occurs when mind and heart agree with the Spirit.

These words are given back to God, released to return to Him in a variety of ways—through prayer, worship and praise, preaching and teaching, writing and singing, and the manner in which we live. It is a continuous return that gives back to God pressed down, shaken together and running over. Revelation is an investment of God into a human being, and He wants a return on it—hundredfold, sixtyfold, or thirtyfold.

Your return depends on how much your mind and heart has successfully combined. We must prove the will of God not only for ourselves personally, but also for the Church corporately. The will of God is changing; the nature of God is constant. Don't confuse the two. We must move forward but we must stay in the Spirit. Whatever we know about God, whatever we understand or have experienced of Him, it has probably not prepared us for what He is about to do! He is building a new prototype of Church to cure our insignificance, our uselessness, and our powerless state. He is changing our structure, renewing our practice of Church, and overhauling our tactic in order to restore us back to our primitive roots.

Cultural relevance is about the Church relating to the language and culture of Heaven, not about making ourselves understood by the world. The world and religion will never understand us. We should never attempt to force understanding to those whom don't understand.

Power breaks through! We spend time, energy, and resources to present God in a modern way to a sophisticated society, and then wonder why the effort and produces such an insufficient return. The manifest presence of God can do more in one moment than we can do in weeks of activity. The Great Commission is better and more easily fulfilled by a people who are God-conscious in mind and heart, totally sold out to His life, love, and purpose. Think about that. If we are in total agreement with what God is doing we will see breakthrough.

Has your thinking been endorsed by the Spirit of God? Is it okay for you to think the way that you do currently? What is the effect of your current thought-life on your holiness, integrity, faith, relationship with God, harmony with people, witness in the world, understanding of the Word, and practical relevance of the church in vision and operation?

Does God want us to break out of our current thought pattern about church into a new expression? If we always do what we have always done, then we'll always have what we've always got…which is insane! Have we submitted our current thought processes to God so that He is free to interfere with our mind-set to bring change?

By this, we do not mean just a mental agreement in the direction of God's right to change things. Remember, mental renewal begins in the heart—loving God before our own comfort and lifestyle, recognizing that we belong to Him and are His to use how He pleases. With God, it is an affair of the heart first. It's a love relationship that puts our life into His hands on a daily basis. Our mind can play tricks on us if our heart is pretending to love God.

Is our current mind-set preventing us from entering into a fresh experience of God? I have been stupid in this area on many occasions. That is why I can truly be of service to the Body of Christ. We have to have our minds set on things above. I have a history of letting my mind dictate to my heart what it can/cannot believe, think, and do.

My question these days as I hold my life under a microscope at certain times is this: "Is this still okay for You...is my thought-life interfering with something You want to show me or speak to me about?"

If we change our mind, He will change our heart. If we change our thinking, He will change our emotions. Fresh experience in our relationship with God alters our perception of spiritual reality at that point and leads to a redirection in our thinking.

As we go through the cycle, we come to a point of transformation where we are ready to go to the next level.

Before I became a Christian, I had a certain mind-set about God, about church, and about the Bible. Experiencing God really blew my mind. I used to think God was just up in Heaven waiting to punish me here on earth for the next thing I did wrong. When I came into a personal experience of God Himself, it altered all the states of my thinking on those levels. I realized that, to become a Christian, I had to change my mind enough to let God come into my life in a fresh way. He broke through the barrier of my thinking to touch my heart. As a non-Christian, I was living out of God's divine order; my heart came after my mind.

Divine order begins with the heart greatest before God. Our relationship with Him is an affair of the heart. Many people become Christians but do not realize that they must maintain the new order. They do not place any emphasis on worship and praise as a primary means of maintaining trust and faith. The mind rules all.

The way we come into salvation is the way that our spiritual journey is governed. Experience God in the heart, bring your mind into joyful submission, and receive a spiritual transformation.

A change of mind-set begins in a loving heart. If we want to be that prototype we must take heed to the transformation of the Mind of Christ.

Chapter Three
Character and Honor

One of the biggest things I've leaned that is necessary for all Christians is God's character. It is so exciting to walk with God, especially through these days of obvious change. Prayers we have prayed are finding answers. Dreams and aspirations are coming alive in our midst. I have never known a time, in my entire walk with the Lord, when His presence has been so profound and tangible. God has been on an acceleration of a progressive move.

His love, kindness, mercy, and generosity are everywhere, it seems. To be able to express love for God in worship is a great honor. The love and affection of Jesus for His Bride is enormous. To be able to return that love to honor His personality and the way He works is a great blessing, one that we do not deserve. To be included by a God who is so inclusive is a great honor. To know what the Lord is building and to be able to place ourselves in His path, so that we are not obstacles to the world of change but participants in His great endeavor—this is our prayer.

It is to perceive the hand of God at work and not spoil it by being carnal minded. We need His wisdom, grace, and truth to touch our Church situation in this time of change.

We must have revelation that provides momentum to the Spirit and a rationale for our thinking. Transition has a character attached to it.

Transition is not just about changes in structure, style, and strategy; it is about diversity into new prototypes as well as conformity into the image and nature of Jesus.

When I first began to fully understand transition was after I had already been through it many times before. I began to seek the Lord to teach about transition in the Waves of Revival at Belleville, IL and all the lessons I learned came forth. I taught six parts over seven hours just on the subject of transition. I am releasing all my findings that are life changing in this book.

There is a provoking of the Spirit on all levels within and around our lives. In transition, the war between the Holy Spirit and the flesh is intensified. We learn how to hunger and thirst after God in a disciplined and not purely spontaneous manner. Transition is about being made uncomfortable by events, as well as being comforted by the Holy Spirit. Transition is about pain, difficulty, and suffering as well as about a new joy and peace in believing. It is about forsaking sin and abandoning oneself to the cause of God. It is about our sacrifice and His glory. Whatever we have to give up is insignificant compared to the majesty and greatness of His presence. Whatever we give of ourselves is returned back to us pressed down, shaken together, and running over. He gives Himself. The prize is to still know Jesus in all His fullness.

When we here it we don't understand. Transition is also about warfare and perseverance; it's standing our ground and discovering Jesus as the Warrior King. It is about perceiving His majesty and supremacy in such a profound way that our life radically changes. We become real warriors, not just weekend soldiers or Sunday fighters. Excitement rises up in worship, and our prayer becomes more enthusiastic.

The temperature is rising. The Holy Spirit is infusing us with a new energy so that we can rise up out of the tiredness we feel. Transition *is* tiring. We need God's power to stand up under it. Transition is about laying down everything we are and taking up everything that He is. Transition is necessary upheaval. It is the passing of one dimension and the release of another. In the difficulty of changing over, we console ourselves with the fact that we asked for all this! Remember all those prayers of "Lord, change us; do something new; pour out Your Spirit in a fresh way. Father, we don't want to be stuck in this place; we want to move on in the Spirit"? Remember those? If you prayed anything remotely like that…it's your fault! You asked for it. What more do you want. We press in for more of God and then all hell breaks loose. After the prayer comes the frustration. This is the irritation, the aggravation that is sent by God to provoke us to more prayer. Frustration is the provocation of God to enforce change quickly. It will not leave us alone; it grips us. It makes us examine the old and explore the new. Frustration is the piece of wood that bridges the gap between two dimensions. We know it is risky. We can go only one step at a time. However, we have found that it is more faith-destroying to stay where we are than to risk the adventure of change. Many never really make it through this. They back off when frustrations come and then even give up. We have to make it through transition or we will keep going around the mountain until we finish transition. Put your foot on the plank and let's go together.

Chapter Four
The New Church

If you have read this far you may be ready for what I'm about to release. There are going to be hundreds of different types of churches, all finding their place together in the Body of Christ. The next dimension is taken up with a very strong Kingdom culture. It is only when we bring the pieces together in a Kingdom setting that we begin to demonstrate that Kingdom desire that sits closer to the heart of God.

Building church without a desire for the Kingdom puts a restraining order on it from Heaven in terms of how far the work can go. If we do not build with Kingdom in mind, then we build something that reflects our own ego. Churches are to be God's Kingdom not ours. What we are constructing has its foundation in empire—a personal domain of the anointed man of God whose own anointing is greater than the church he has built because his people are passive observers of all that God is doing with him.

How boring it is to be part of a church where the anointed one is sold out to his own ministry. In His mercy, the Lord has allowed us time to grow up and work these things through. For far to long it has been all centered round some man pleasing or man lifting up because God has placed a special anointing on a mans life. Listen don't get me wrong there should be respect toward ministers as long as God is being lifted up.

Transition is about the destruction of a empire and the refocus on Kingdom. It is better for us to fall on this rock and be broken and humbled before God than for it to fall upon us and crush all that we have built in the name of Jesus…but with an eye out for ourselves. We must humble ourselves and put everything into His hands so that He can decide whether we are trustworthy. If God did not own the getting of our ministry, He will not own the having of it—not without making Himself unrighteous.

If we cheated others, broke our word, trod on people, used and discarded people, or promoted ourselves to get where we are, we need to repent right quick! We cannot over look these things if we are to rise into this new thing God is doing.

Make restoration where God leads you, because the shaking has already begun. Other churches matter. Even if a Church doesn't believe the way you do it is still connected as part of the Body of Christ. The Kingdom is more important. Establish the Kingdom and build the church, in that order. As you build the church, build Kingdom into your people. Other churches matter. Pray for them; have a heart for their growth. Have a desire to participate in the development of the whole Body of Christ across the whole area.

It will not guarantee revival. However, the water level of the Kingdom will raise enough in our hearts to prevent us from building our own empire, however small. If we plan to be inclusive and work with others where we can, at least know that the Lord will not have to shake or dismantle our work later on. We can build a net between churches and cities. Each church will represent part of that net, a place where certain lines meet and join together. When the net is strong enough to bear the weight of what God wants to do in the Kingdom, we will see some action.

God works according to man's preparation and placement. The early Church was in one place and of one accord when Pentecost came. Can our sense of preparation and placement be any less?

The Lord is sharpening the Church at this time. He is putting a cutting edge on what we are doing. He is raising up a prophetic Church, one that is led by every word out of His mouth. It is a Church led by the Spirit, not one necessarily with systems, zones, or management strategies. The ministry of the Church will reflect God's relaxed but disciplined approach. On the surface it looks chaotic, because God is not a manager; He is a facilitator. Underneath the action, though, there is a calm order that arises out of God's character and nature. Many leaders are not restful people. They are activity-oriented, or managerially productive. The basis of order comes from within. It is the anointing to be at rest, calm, and peaceful before God and man. When God is in the driver's seat, all things will work out. It is the capacity to step back into God in times of tension and trouble, to know His rest and peace. The work of the church is full of the tension of many differences in ministry, many different people, and many contrasting applications of gifting. The capacity for chaos is endless. A little organization around this is fine. We need enough strategy to keep things moving in broadly the right direction. Too much organization will stifle creativity, spontaneity, and initiative. Organization may create order in the world of business, education, and research, but it does not create order in the church. The church is a supernatural body, one where the chain of command is less obvious.

It is the goal of leadership to teach everyone how to hear God's voice and to be led by the Spirit. It is the goal of leadership to train, equip, empower, and release the saints into the work of the ministry. It is the goal of leadership to follow after God so closely themselves that they become a model, a pattern, and an example worth following. It is the goal of leadership to facilitate, through friendship and trust, a proper framework for accountability that is powerful and relational without being based on some armed forces structure. It is the goal of leadership to produce whole, healthy Christians who can take initiative, be led by the Spirit, and cause the enemy endless trouble. If our structure and chain of command is too rigid, we make it easy for the enemy to stop us from being effective.

If the enemy opposes one part, another part rises up. When persecuted in one area, we rise up elsewhere; when attacked in one spot, we pop up somewhere else; when opposed in that part, we return to the first place and start again.

In the church, too much order removes the supernatural edge that truly confounds the devil. Too much order makes us predictable and very, very ordinary. If things are running to smooth then to say it plain, you are dead or in a dead place.

If our people spend more time learning about order, structure, who to report to, how to make referrals, chains of command, and accountable organizational behavior, they will not develop the initiative, creativity, order, and spontaneity of the Holy Spirit. We all finally are getting the understanding of submitting to leadership before doing something in meetings but now we must get the leadership to submit to the Holy Spirit. What happens when a leader does not submit to the Holy Spirit is we will have a man-centered ministry, not a Spirit-led one. I like organization. I believe in structure. However, I would love for more leaders to be restful, peaceful, facilitating, trusting, and calm individuals in God, so that they can operate these things properly.

If we want the approval of God, we will have to face the annoyance of the world. The new prototype of church will anger the world. They will preach at us in anger because we have dared to go back to our roots. They like us to be familiar and predictable.

Obviously, familiarity is good when it relates to the character of the church—their kindnesses, goodness, love of people, mercy, and reliability. People should be able to count on the nature of the church being one with the character of our Lord. However, in many places the church has become an institution of convenience. We give but we have no voice. We can comfort but we cannot challenge. We are seen but are not heard. Open-mindedness has been stretched to embrace sin—to cover it without dealing with it. We do not have the disapproval or enmity of the world; we have their mockery and contempt. There is a new prototype of church emerging that will clash with the world and Religious Christianity.

A prototype is the first in a series. The Church will rediscover her radical edge, but not by playing with the world's toys and using them differently. Real radical behavior in church is grounded in the supernatural. It proceeds from the mouth of God; it emanates from simple obedience to His ways; it emerges out of Holy Spirit boldness to follow the plans of God with fervent faith. It is to be willing to look foolish in order to confound the world. We all will be pioneers in this next move of God.

His plans for our churches will mean profound changes to the structure, vision, personality, and effectiveness of our meetings, missions, training, and discipleship forums. We will see a radical change in leadership style and method. When building a prototype church, all our mistakes are public.

One thing we should note here: Real pioneers do not criticize other pioneers because they know how hard it can be to build something new. Settlers usually make the most vicious of critics. They haven't done it themselves and have no intention of taking what they perceive to be insane risks. Their ideas are that it is better to snipe from the sidelines and then borrow the new thing once it has been proven. Some even argue that it is their "refining" comments that have played a valuable part in maturing the original concept.

I guess we will find out what the Lord thinks of this type of behavior on the Day of Judgment. Sadly for some, they will probably reap from what they have sown a little earlier than they would like. When we go through times of testing with our new prototype, we will have an audience of both well-wishers and critics. Many critics have no honor and less mercy. It is true that the design stages will be filled with problems. Our raw material is people. Some can stand the strain and stress; others are caught out by the sacrifice and hard work. No one likes to fail. However, it is not all about success or failure, but primarily about learning and growing. It is about pressing on through the disappointments. It is about believing in the vision God has given and learning how not to do something before it suddenly clicks into place. To be a warrior you must finish transition.

The Lord does not measure success by results, but rather by the faithfulness we display toward Him and His vision. Pioneering is about faithfulness to the call God has given us. Many of us are faithful only to ourselves. Self-preservation will always separate the true pioneers from those who progress only at other people's expense. Some prototype churches will have a broad base of ministry; others will have a narrow field of operation.

Some will look after several people-groups; others may base their ministry around one type. I know churches that cater for such groups as youth, people on the drug scene, and people of a certain nationality or economic type. It is exciting to see the many flavors that exist in the wider Body of Christ.

True spiritual conformity is only ever about being made over in the image of the Lord Jesus Christ. Jesus came to put a face on God.

John 14:9 Jesus saith unto him, Have I been so long time with you, and yet hast thou not known me, Philip? he that hath seen me hath seen the Father; and how sayest thou *then,* Shew us the Father?

Christ wants to show Himself to us and through us. We are here to put a face on Christ. By our character, we demonstrate His nature. The operation of the Church in ministry must reveal all the creative diversity in the heart of God.

The broad dimension of anointing in the Holy Spirit cannot be contained within a single church, network, or organization. We must love and appreciate different ministries and befriend one another to help, shape, and support the full work of the Kingdom through the Church. This is strategies to building a prototype Church.

CHAPTER FIVE
The Inner Channel

I am interested in what works and what is beautiful. The Church is a paradox. We are supposed to be God's hoses or inner channels of His Holy Spirit power. In other words His Glory shall flow through us like a watering hose.

It is not what the world thinks it is. It is contrary to received conventional opinion. Sadly, that also may be true for large sections of the Church.

The Church is a house and a city, an army and a bride, a building and a body. Each of these concepts is designed to shake us and stretch our thinking and practice beyond our current capacity. Most of the ways that God operates are absurd. His ways are not ours and His thoughts are radically different from our own.

Isaiah 55:8, 9 For my thoughts *are* not your thoughts, neither *are* your ways my ways, saith the LORD. For *as* the heavens are higher than the earth, so are my ways higher than your ways, and my thoughts than your thoughts.

Everything He does is to display His glory and majesty. He is not seeking a powerful people to represent Him. Rather He looks for all those who are weak, foolish, despised, and written off; and He inhabits them with His own strength. He has not come to give strength but to be strength to us as we relate to Him in weakness. He fills everything with Himself. Many who are in leadership may be passed over because they don't need God as the nameless and faceless do. Most leaders today could do ministry without God for years and no one would notice. If there is no prophetic, healings, miracles and power of God, where is God?

He is our joy, our righteousness, and the power of salvation. That means we must understand the difference between vulnerability and insecurity. All God's dealings with us are to create maximum dependence upon Him. He calls us to do the impossible. He demands that we see what is invisible. He thrusts us into situations that would overwhelm us.

Insecurity produces unbelief. A paralysis occurs where there needs to be movement and faith in action. People see their own smallness rather than the majesty of God. This is why we must keep our focus past the flesh and on God.

Numbers 13:33 And there we saw the giants, the sons of Anak, *which come* of the giants: and we were in our own sight as grasshoppers, and so we were in their sight.

Some people are prevented from achieving breakthrough because they cannot translate their weakness into power.

Vulnerability knows that God is happy to send us out as lambs amongst wolves because He is hugely confident in His own ability to watch over us and work through our weaknesses. When we are vulnerable, we see our inadequacies in the light of God's sovereignty and power, and we discover hope and faith. Like Paul, we rejoice in our weaknesses that the power of Christ may rest upon us.

2Corinthians 12:9, 10 And he said unto me, My grace is sufficient for thee: for my strength is made perfect in weakness. Most gladly therefore will I rather glory in my infirmities, that the power of Christ may rest upon me. Therefore I take pleasure in infirmities, in reproaches, in necessities, in persecutions, in distresses for Christ's sake: for when I am weak, then am I strong.

The whole point of vulnerability is to bring us to a place of restful dependence in a powerful and overcoming God. Vulnerability is given by God to release His presence, which builds self-esteem and confidence in God's sovereignty. Insecurity occurs when the enemy twists our soul to reduce our self-esteem and cause us to focus on our shortcomings.

Chapter Six
What Are We Giving Birth To?

God looks for a catalyst among His people—someone who will enter into a determined relationship with Him and who is capable of suspending disbelief as he discovers the majesty of God. There is a remnant of people with this kind of hunger. The Lord is always on a treasure hunt, finding something precious in the unlikeliest of places! We look at the flesh of a vessel; God sees the treasure. We are more concerned with the rubbish it is buried in than the natural value of the real find itself. We see the rough edges; He sees the cut and polished jewel. Thank God for Jesus!

I love the way that God esteems us in Christ...the way He cherishes the bride in us...the value that He places on our lives because of His Son. He always sees the treasure within and then works to extract the precious from the worthless. Humans do the opposite. We take the worthless away from what is precious. Our focus is on rubbish removal and not on the glory of the Christ-life that is present though hidden in every believer.

I am a living testimony of God looking beyond the outside of myself and seeing something that I didn't even see. There was a treasure hidden underneath all of my shortcomings. Trust me I had more than most people and God still saw something in me.

God always speaks to our potential while simultaneously showing us Himself. I AM, is with you! Gideon was a frightened, inadequate, resentful, questioning, and angry young man with severe low self-esteem. God looked beyond all that and spoke to the hidden capacity that was hidden within the man.

He said, "The Lord is with you, mighty warrior"

In the face of Gideon's initial alarm, He would only restate: "I will be with you!" God did not deal with Gideon's inadequacies. The Lord established the warrior in him by showing Gideon His own nature and sovereignty.

Whatever we speak into people will rise up, for good or for bad. Speak to the flesh and it will bite you. Speak to the Christ-life and it will bless you. Always speak to what is noble in people and nobility will emerge. If you can look in the Spirit and speak as God sees them.

When I prophesy to an individual, I may see many things that would say that this Word I'm giving them will never come to pass. Let me tell you if God only spoke and used people who appeared ready in the flesh there wouldn't be many ministers today.

The Holy Spirit is present in people, so if we speak to the fruit of His character and not to our misgivings or suspicion about them, we will save both ourselves and others from bitter confusion and possible rejection.

God will inhabit only what is compatible with His purpose. He comes to tell us that there is a new way of looking, being, walking, and doing. The Lord is not coming to do what we want but to fulfill His desires. It is vital that we be ready to pursue God's desire.

The Lord lives only with what is pure, holy, and consecrated. He cohabits with the virgins who have jars of oil. We are in a season of grace where God is covering us to give us time to repent. How will God come to you? He will come in mercy, because of your desire for Him, or in judgment because of His desire for you?

We want to be a dwelling place of God by the Spirit and therefore compatible to the image of God. He is compatible with humility and brokenness. He gives grace to the humble. Grace is His empowering presence flowing out from the crucible of brokenness and humility.

We are a people seeking identification with God through crucifixion, humility, servanthood, obedience, and suffering; having the same mind in us that Jesus had in His compatibility.

How desperate are we to be a dwelling place of God in our lifestyles? People must have a goal for sanctification. Sanctification is not necessarily coming to a place where we never sin but to a place where the practice of sin is not normal. Sanctification precedes revival.

We need teachers and prophets combining together in the process of sanctification, acting to deliver a purity that will bless the Lord. Many charismatics do not know the difference between legalism and self-discipline. There have not been the truths being released such as sins in a person's life. Leaders today need to be a preacher of truth. Repent for the Kingdom of God is at hand.

Real accountability is provoked and promotes self-control, a fruit of the Spirit. Imposed accountability is dealt from above and can produce shame, fear, and apathy as well as controlling, domineering leadership. God is raising up a new kind of leader that will be able to preach and release a real spirit of fear of the Lord.

Chapter Seven
Who Are the Helpers of God?

What do we want out of life in the Church? What kind of house are we building and what type of wineskin do we want? Who are the external catalysts and builders who can shape our design and destiny?

Who are the internal movers and shakers who will respond to what the Spirit is saying to the churches? God is asking these questions to all of us today.

Who are the people who can be positive agents for change just by the quality of their life in the Lord? The womb represents a place of growth and stretching as the life within takes shape.

Every church has a womb. Some churches are capable of giving birth to multiple life forms; others are able to deliver a single aspect of vision. Some churches cannot conceive while others cannot produce. I'll keep saying things many different ways so that it gets clear what God is looking for in us.

Every church needs a helper who can deliver the vision into a specific form capable of interacting with God and humanity.

In Scripture, the helpers of God are the fivefold ministries mentioned in Ephesians 4. They are given as gifts to train, equip, empower, and release the Body of Christ into ministry. There is a greater depth of spiritual reality that emerges in the combined company of apostles and prophets. This is a must in the Church God is raising up.

New foundations have to be laid if we are restructuring the building for a different use or a more dynamic purpose. Apostles and prophets are the only ministries that can release the dynamic of the presence of God that turns a church from an organization to an organism. We cannot do it without the Apostles and Prophets as the foundation of the Church.

The church must become cloud-sensitive, not crowd-sensitive. The new wineskin must be defined prophetically. The new structure of the church requires apostolic strategy. Many churches have become a memorial to what God did.

Raising up and renewing the prophetic in our midst will enable us to preserve the revelation that will rebuild the house and keep the wineskin soft. We can pass on our church style or we can release prophetic successors. To do the latter, we need the Father's touch as a wise master-builder.

Good leadership releases the fruit of the Holy Spirit in the lives of people by continually encouraging the flock back into the arms of Jesus. Apostles are the Believers of the church sent out to prepare a Bride for the Son.

We must distinguish between leadership of the church and management. Leaders are proficient in the art of going somewhere and taking people with them. Managers maintain what they have. Leaders go out to get something more. They know they have to give something to gain something more.

Many churches are not built for the battleground. If we are truly walking with Jesus, then we will partake of all the warfare that He provokes.

Luke 22:28 Ye are they which have continued with me in my temptations.

We must be ready for the storm that is to come. The anointing of the fivefold ministries are to add layer upon layer to the revelation and release of a warrior bride.

The most critical part of this is that the Church has rejected the Apostles and Prophets when it is vital in this hour to have them both firmly in place.

I need to be brief and to the point. The principle I want to operate from is this: The fivefold ministries are sent by the Lord not necessarily to *do* the job, but specifically to train and equip the Body of Christ to fulfill God's purposes through grassroots body ministry.

So I am going to put their ministry into a realistic context of apostolic practice.

I am using the word *apostolic* as an umbrella term to indicate the function of all the fivefold ministries operating together in the life of a church.

Apostolic ministry operates according to the measure of the grace gift given by Christ. Some of the main ingredients of apostolic ministry are for...

- Perfecting and maturing the saints.
- Edifying and building up the Body of Christ.
- Producing saints for the effective work of the ministry.
- Bringing the saints into a unity of the faith.
- Creating knowledge of the Son of God to produce a perfect man.
- Attaining the measure of the stature of Christ's fullness.
- Raising spiritual children to adulthood.

Ephesians 2:19-22 Now therefore ye are no more strangers and foreigners, but fellowcitizens with the saints, and of the household of God; And are built upon the foundation of the apostles and prophets, Jesus Christ himself being the chief corner *stone;* In whom all the building fitly framed together groweth unto an holy temple in the Lord: In whom ye also are builded together for an habitation of God through the Spirit.

Ephesians 4:11-16 And he gave some, apostles; and some, prophets; and some, evangelists; and some, pastors and teachers; For the perfecting of the saints, for the work of the ministry, for the edifying of the body of Christ: Till we all come in the unity of the faith, and of the knowledge of the Son of God, unto a perfect man, unto the measure of the stature of the fulness of Christ: That we *henceforth* be no more children, tossed to and fro, and carried about with every wind of doctrine, by the sleight of men, *and* cunning craftiness, whereby they lie in wait to deceive; But speaking the truth in love, may grow up into him in all things, which is the head, *even* Christ: From whom the whole body fitly joined together and compacted by that which every joint supplieth, according to the effectual working in the measure of every part, maketh increase of the body unto the edifying of itself in love.

Colossians 1:25-29 Whereof I am made a minister, according to the dispensation of God which is given to me for you, to fulfil the word of God; *Even* the mystery which hath been hid from ages and from generations, but now is made manifest to his saints: To whom God would make known what *is* the riches of the glory of this mystery among the Gentiles; which is Christ in you, the hope of glory: Whom we preach, warning every man, and teaching every man in all wisdom; that we may present every man perfect in Christ Jesus: Whereunto I also labour, striving according to his working, which worketh in me mightily.

Hebrews 6:1, 2 Therefore leaving the principles of the doctrine of Christ, let us go on unto perfection; not laying again the foundation of repentance from dead works, and of faith toward God, Of the doctrine of baptisms, and of laying on of hands, and of resurrection of the dead, and of eternal judgment.

Apostles are father figures who produce quality leaders who, in turn, nurture and strengthen the flock.

They are wise master builders who lay the correct spiritual foundations. They will ensure that the Church is built on the sure foundation of Jesus Christ.

The Church is in a Season of Profound of Change

1Corinthians 3:9-16 For we are labourers together with God: ye are God's husbandry, *ye are* God's building. According to the grace of God which is given unto me, as a wise masterbuilder, I have laid the foundation, and another buildeth thereon. But let every man take heed how he buildeth thereupon. For other foundation can no man lay than that is laid, which is Jesus Christ. Now if any man build upon this foundation gold, silver, precious stones, wood, hay, stubble; Every man's work shall be made manifest: for the day shall declare it, because it shall be revealed by fire; and the fire shall try every man's work of what sort it is. If any man's work abide which he hath built thereupon, he shall receive a reward. If any man's work shall be burned, he shall suffer loss: but he himself shall be saved; yet so as by fire. Know ye not that ye are the temple of God, and *that* the Spirit of God dwelleth in you?

The Church is built upon the apostles and prophets relating to Jesus as the Chief Cornerstone.

In bringing change that confirms the new vision and direction the apostle may, where necessary, give input to the restructuring of the leadership. New foundations may need to be re-laid to enable us to overcome the roots of our history. New beginnings are a powerful motivator to a Church going through a profound season of change. There is a dynamic in the corporate life of a church that simply does not exist in one's personal life. We must ensure that our leaders can cope effectively with the corporate stress of a company of people engaged in active service. It is not the title that people give to themselves that defines who they are; it is the fruit of what they produce. Apostles have a concern for the house of God, particularly in relation to people being fitted and framed together. Relational church is vital.

As the work grows, apostles set in place a leadership that will represent the oversight and that will effectively produce the quality people required for the coming days. They develop the partnerships that are required to run the local church and the wider vision of the corporate Body of Christ in the area. Apostles are Kingdom people concerned with the whole Church in the region, not just their particular network's representative. Apostles provide the culture and the atmosphere of the church by the way they relate to leaders and by the way those leaders are trained to relate to the church. Apostles are facilitators enabling good communication and the growing of the vision from the ground up, not the top down.

Many churches today have been established without Apostles and Prophets. They are sending ministries, releasing others into specific times of building and blessing within the local church. Everyone who is sent in with the next building block is a representative figure of that apostolic character and strategy.

The chief role of a *prophet* is not to prophesy. It is to teach everyone how to hear the voice of God themselves. We want everyone to be trained effectively in hearing the voice of the Lord and in distinguishing between that, their own opinions, and the disrupting influence of the enemy.

The setting of protocol as a framework for moving in revelatory prophecy in the church is extremely vital. There is a huge difference between the simple inspirational prophecy that exhorts, edifies, and comforts.

1Corinthians 14:1-5 Follow after charity, and desire spiritual *gifts,* but rather that ye may prophesy. For he that speaketh in an *unknown* tongue speaketh not unto men, but unto God: for no man understandeth *him;* howbeit in the spirit he speaketh mysteries. But he that prophesieth speaketh unto men *to* edification, and exhortation, and comfort. He that speaketh in an *unknown* tongue edifieth himself; but he that prophesieth edifieth the church. I would that ye all spake with tongues, but rather that ye prophesied: for greater *is* he that prophesieth than he that speaketh with tongues, except he interpret, that the church may receive edifying.

The former can be given a fairly free hand because it is highly unlikely anyone will be damaged or upset by inspirational prophecy. At its heart is a desire to bless, encourage, support, and build up the people around us. The worst that may happen is that we get a blessing in an area of our lives that does not exactly need one!

The latter, however, may be incredibly damaging and hurtful if we do not set appropriate guidelines.

Revelatory prophecy may lead us across governmental boundaries in church life that are inappropriate and unscriptural. Whatever we hear from the Lord that is of a revelatory nature must be shared with the leadership first. There is a governmental principle at stake. The operation of certain spiritual gifts often requires defined cooperation and relationship with the leadership of the work. Prophets promote such partnerships. We must keep everything prophetically released aligned with the Word of God. They also help to create a framework for ongoing development of prophetic people. We want leaders willing and able to pastor the prophetic, not merely regulate the ministry.

Ongoing training in the gift, the ministry, and the office of a prophet can be laid down over a period of many years. It can take between 10 and 15 years to make a prophet, depending on his access to a good prophet/teacher who can model and mentor him effectively. Without that key person in place, many people will never make it or will take twice the time. Today God is doing an acceleration of this time frame. So if someone really allows God to bring them into the Office it could be a much shorter time.

A prophet will prophesy and model how the gift should be correctly used. There are too many blessing prophets and not enough of the building type in today's Church. Blessing prophets do a good job in onetime situations by preaching and ministering prophetically to people.

They do not, however, leave a deposit in terms of raising up a local team of prophetic people who can be trained and discipled in the gift and ministry. They do it *for* you rather than teaching you how to do it!

I have heard many leaders over the years put down prophetic ministry. The usual comment is that they were good, the meetings were exciting, but there was little lasting fruit. The other main criticism is that some of the prophetic words never come to pass.

All personal prophecy is conditional. If we obey the Lord and live in the truth of Scripture, then God's word—prophetic or otherwise—will come to pass. The truth will set us free—if we live in it and depend on God. If we do not, if we sin, then the truth cannot set us free.

I have sat in many leaders' groups and heard their horror stories about prophetic ministry. I have acted as a troubleshooter between the prophetic and other ministries. I have campaigned for the prophetic ministry to get its house in order. This is one of the reasons why I wrote "Increasing Your Prophetic Gift and Receiving Personal Prophecy" to be tools to help people understand the prophetic ministry. I have unraveled problems with prophetic people for many years. I have also sat with prophets and heard their horror stories of being treated like magicians, being put into situations and expected to pull rabbits out of hats. Even in the beginning of my own prophetic ministry many would thank me for the reading or even ask me to speak to their dead pets or relatives. This is more of the psychic abominations from the pit of hell. The Church needs to get a clear picture concerning the subject of prophetic and prophecy.

People think that prophets can cure years of bad leadership, abuse of power, lack of vision, and lack of development with a few meetings and some choice prophetic words.

The best way to ensure a person's failure in God would be to make sure that…

- We did not insist on biblical foundations in doctrine and practice.
- We failed to marry training with discipleship.
- We never created opportunities to serve.
- We impose vision and accountability onto people rather than inspire its growth from below.
- We never give loving, effective feedback to people.

- Our leaders are not mentored into becoming fathers and facilitators.
- The majesty and sovereignty of God is not magnified in the hearts of key people (we model what we move in). I am quite sure that we could all add to the list. An example of doctrine and practicality working together would be the following:

Practical: "Stand firm against the enemy". This is a wonderful command! But how can we practice this if we do not understand the doctrinal truth of...

Ephesians 2:6 And hath raised *us* up together, and made *us* sit together in heavenly *places* in Christ Jesus:

Doctrine precedes practice. So the truth of being victoriously raised in Christ precedes power over the enemy.

In the violence of spiritual confrontation with an relentless enemy, the assurance of our position in Christ enables us to make a firm stand.

Apostles send out evangelists, pastors, teachers, and prophets to provide building blocks to train and equip the Body of Christ. They are advisor ministries to enable the development of leaders, key people, and church members with an anointed lifestyle. They stand in the gap between where the church is now and where it needs to be, assisting people into new levels of strategic growth, anointing, and spiritual power. They facilitate the growth and development of the church in ministry and mission. They train people for the battlefield. They magnify Jesus to the Church and the world at large. They live by example, modeling all that God has bestowed on them in ways that are revelatory, faith-filled, and full of integrity. True Apostles today should live a life of Godly character and walking in the power of miracles, signs and wonders.

Chapter Eight
Dreams & Interpretation of Dreams

In Building a Prototype Church we must clear up some of the things concerning one of the most powerful ways God speaks to us and that is dreams and interpretation. This chapter is based on my experiences of being around many ministers who interpret dreams. We need the truth to be set free of all the false teaching concerning that we can interpret dreams to mean the same symbols all the time. I'm talking about this symbol means this and this symbol means that. I have even talked personally with some authors of dream books and they said they don't even use their own guidelines to interpret dreams. Dreams and interpretation must stay inline with the Word of God. There are some good books out there but I have spent the best part of ten years seeking God on this life changing subject.

Dreams can seem complex and confusing although usually they are not. To help simplify them, I have divided them into two categories: miscellaneous dreams and message dreams. Our focus will be on message dreams; however, we will give a few details regarding miscellaneous dreams as well.

To help understand message dreams, we have divided them into types: *objective*, *subjective*, and *combination* dreams. Each dream type is given for specific purposes.

Miscellaneous Dreams

One of the first skills we need to learn is to distinguish miscellaneous dreams from message dreams and then to ignore them. That skill comes from knowing there is a difference and by evaluating each dream as it comes. In other words, we learn to differentiate by experience. The majority of our miscellaneous dreams are "natural process dreams."

Natural Process Dreams

Many of the dreams we dream will be natural process dreams, also referred to as "random neuron firings" in the brain. Everyone has these dreams, and, in fact, research has concluded that preventing people from having these dreams for more than a few days will cause them to begin to show signs of mental breakdown. If that is the case (and we have no reason to disagree), we all must dream, and those dreams we call natural process dreams.

We do not believe these dreams carry any particular message. We like to think of them as mental "defragments". Although they have a function in our health and mental wellbeing, they usually lack the clarity and direction we look for in message dreams.

Attempting to understand these natural process dreams as significant in our lives can lead to frustration, "Practical Dreaming," and to the eventual disregard of all dreams.

Body/Chemical Dreams

The body is a mixture of many chemicals. When the body experiences illness or fever, dreams seem to reflect the conflict within. Legal drugs, illegal drugs, or alcohol can also affect dreams, even to the point of becoming nightmares as the body withdraws from the drug.

Pregnancy is a time when the chemicals and hormones of the body are doing strange and wondrous things. This can affect dreams.

Seductive Dreams

This dream type does not fit well under the heading of "miscellaneous dreams" but is experienced by many.

In response to those who have had this experience. Not to be confused with what we often call nightmares, these dreams are under the influence of the demonic—referred to as incubus and seductive spirits.

Because this is a sensitive area with potential for embarrassment, people usually do not talk openly about this type of dream.

Incubus and *seductive* spirits in dreams are defined as follows: incubus (noun; pl. *incubi*) a male demon believed to have sexual intercourse with sleeping women; seductive (noun; pl. *succubi*) a female demon believed to have sexual intercourse with sleeping men.

Incubus: demon in male form that seeks to have sexual intercourse with sleeping women; the corresponding spirit in female form is called a seductive.

People have been violated in this way, not knowing the source of these dreamlike experiences.

Until I learned of these spirits, I thought the experience was just a natural process dream I had to endure, and these dreams occurred many times over the years. After coming to an understanding of their source, I had a reoccurrence of this type of dream and commanded the spirit to leave in the name of Jesus. The dream ended immediately. If, using this approach, the dream does not end immediately—as it must if it is demonic—treat the dream as any other with symbolism that needs to be understood.

False Dreams

A person can misuse a dream knowingly or unknowingly for self-serving purposes. Scripture warns us about this.

Jeremiah 23:32 Behold, I *am* against them that prophesy false dreams, saith the LORD, and do tell them, and cause my people to err by their lies, and by their lightness; yet I sent them not, nor commanded them: therefore they shall not profit this people at all, saith the LORD.

Zechariah 10:2 For the idols have spoken vanity, and the diviners have seen a lie, and have told false dreams; they comfort in vain: therefore they went their way as a flock, they were troubled, because *there was* no shepherd.

We should evaluate all dreams against the truths of Scripture. Respond cautiously to the message of any dream. God can confirm a message in a variety of ways, dreams being only one.

Message Dreams

When mentioning dreams it can be understood that I'm referring to message dreams which are the focus of my attention.

Message dreams usually have clarity and a sense of purpose to them. These are the dreams the Father gives to communicate with us. To help understand our dreams, divide them into two distinct types and a combined type by determining who the dream is for.

Subjective and Objective Dreams

To properly understand and respond to our message dreams, it is imperative to know if the dream is for the dreamer (subjective) or for someone else (objective). The concept of using the activity of the dreamer in the dream as the determining factor for subjective/objective dream types has strong support when tested

Building a Prototype Church

against the dreams in the Bible.

- Genesis 15:1–21—God and Abraham; subjective; correct
- Genesis 20:1–18—God and Abimelech; subjective; correct
- Genesis 28:10–22—God to Jacob; subjective; correct
- Genesis 31:10–29—Jacob and God; subjective; correct
- Genesis 37:1–11—Joseph's dreams; combination; correct
- Genesis 40:1–23—Cupbearer and baker; subjective; correct
- Genesis 41:1–49—Pharaoh's dream ; objective; correct
- Genesis 46:1–7—Israel talking with God; subjective; correct
- Judges 7:9–18—Barley loaf dream; objective; correct
- 1 Kings 3:5–28—Solomon dream; subjective; correct
- Daniel 2:1–49—Statue hit by stone; objective; correct
- Daniel 4:4–37—Tree cut down; combination; correct
- Daniel 7:1–28—Four beast from the sea; objective; correct
- Daniel 8:1–27—Ram and goat; objective; correct
- Daniel 10:1–12: ch13—Terrifying vision; objective; correct
- Matthew 1:20–25—God spoke to Joseph; subjective; correct
- Matthew 2:3–15—God spoke to Joseph; subjective; correct
- Matthew 2:19–23—God spoke to Joseph; subjective; correct
- Acts 10:9–16—Peter's animals; subjective; correct
- Acts 16:9—Paul's Macedonian man; subjective; correct

This should instill some confidence in using this approach. We have used this method for many years and appreciate its simplicity in differentiating between subjective, objective, and combination dreams.

Subjective Dreams

A subjective dream is given to the dreamer for the dreamer and about the dreamer. Unless you have a calling to the office of prophet or have the gift of prophecy, most (ninety to ninety five percent) of your dreams are of this type. The main characteristic of this type of dream is that you play an active part in it.

Examples of this type of dream include those of the Pharaoh's baker and cupbearer. In each of their dreams, they played an active role in the dream.

Objective Dreams

An objective dream is given to the dreamer but is not exclusively for the dreamer. The objective dream is one in which the dreamer stands as an observer and does not anticipate in the activities but watches the events unfold.

Examples of this include Daniel's dream of the four beasts coming out of the sea and Pharaoh's dream of the cows and the corn.

In each of these examples, the dreamer was an observer only. Those called to prophetic offices or gifted in prophecy may experience more of this type of dream.

Numbers 12:6 And he said, Hear now my words: If there be a prophet among you, *I* the LORD will make myself known unto him in a vision, *and* will speak unto him in a dream.

Ephesians 4:11, 12 And he gave some, apostles; and some, prophets; and some, evangelists; and some, pastors and teachers; For the perfecting of the saints, for the work of the ministry, for the edifying of the body of Christ:

What does one do when given this type of dream? Some big responsibilities go with the objective dream. Of Daniel, we read that he kept the dream to himself. Later, regarding another dream, he was told to keep it a secret. The apostle John was told to write his vision in a book and send it to the seven churches in Asia Minor, and, with no copier, making seven copies was no small task.

God will make clear to you what you are to do with a dream that pertains to some other person or to the Church. Seek the counsel of one in authority over you before acting, even when there appears to be a clear directive from God. If there is no clear directive, do nothing except to pray into the dream. God shared with Abraham his intentions for Sodom and Gomorrah.

Abraham took on the role of intercessor on behalf of those affected—his nephew Lot and family.

Whether by directive or intercession, we must act with discretion, in humility, and in love.

Not all dreams of those called to be prophets will be of the objective type. Rather, many or most of their dreams will be subjective. As we learn to understand our dreams, as we grow proficient in our dream language, and as we show ourselves faithful in the little things, this may change.

Combination Dreams

There may be an occasional dream wherein you have distinct combination of activity and observation scenes. These dreams may be indicative of an objective dream whose sphere of influence includes you to some degree.

Joseph's dream of his brother's sheaves bowing to his is an example of this. In the early part of the dream, he says, "*we were binding sheaves in the field*" which notes a brief period of activity on Joseph's part, but, in the remainder and larger portion of the dream, his role was an observer. The message of the dream was about his brothers, but it also affected him.

Purposes of Dreams

All message dreams, whether subjective, objective, or combination have purpose and are profitable for our use.

Paul tells us the Bible is "inspired" of God, or "God breathed" (*theopneustos*)—the literal meaning of the Greek word used by the apostle in the following verse:

2Timothy 3:16 All scripture *is* given by inspiration of God, and *is* profitable for doctrine, for reproof, for correction, for instruction in righteousness:

How much of the interaction between a parent and child is covered under these same themes? My experiences with dreams have found these to be foundational to their function. Dreams are also given to encourage and as an expression of God's love to us. In the interpretation of dreams, a key principle is that the understanding and interpretation must be in agreement with the teaching and intent of Scripture.

For example, the correct interpretation of a dream would never suggest you harm, defraud, or slander a person. These actions are contrary to the command to love one another as we love ourselves. The interpretation of any dream should never contradict God's Word.

No doubt this list is not exhaustive, but it may help in understanding the dreams we have.

Work dreams

God has a plan for our lives much the same as his statement toward the nation of Israel in,

Jeremiah 29:11 For I know the thoughts that I think toward you, saith the LORD, thoughts of peace, and not of evil, to give you an expected end.

In the interpretation of dreams, a key principle is that the understanding and interpretation must be in agreement with the teaching and intent of Scripture. This also is concerning that certain symbols mean something in a dream. If there is no real scriptural basis then the symbols interpretation may be wrong. The Holy Spirit is our interpreter.

He will instruct us in the work or call he has for our lives as we follow him. This may also include an understanding of our gifts and anointing. In essence, he tells us his plan and purpose for our lives in a vocation dream. This is often done one step at a time.

Too often we are tempted, after receiving a "call," to run out and begin the work. The calling is not the commissioning, so wait for the commissioning before you act.

The Apostle Paul spent three years in Arabia, three years in the "*regions of Syria and Cilicia,*" and one year in Antioch with Barnabas before he was commissioned to do the work of his calling by the Holy Spirit. It was many years after his anointing before David became king of Israel. Do you remember Moses' forty years of training as a leader of large flocks before his commissioning at the burning bush? Our goal must be to follow the Lord, not to run ahead of him.

Cleansing Dreams

We live in an imperfect world, full of spiritual stench, and we are susceptible to picking up "spiritual stuff" just by being out in our normal day. This can occur unknowingly, while walking through a market place, being in the workplace or traveling and so on. Images, sounds, smells, and so on, may have an effect on us and need to be cleansed from our minds and bodies.

Cleansing dreams are a way of removing from us the effects of the day. This can happen through many situations. The dream just washes everything away that is needed.

Warning Dreams

Warning dreams exhort us not to do certain things and they sometimes tell us the consequences if we continue.

There was a certain woman in the Church who had a seducing spirit. My wife had multiple dreams of her trying to get close to me. She did start to in a very vague way but because of the dream I sought the Lord and knew it was time to keep a closer guard. Thank you Lord because I am not going to assume that I'm strong when the warning alarms keep coming.

Genesis 20:3 But God came to Abimelech in a dream by night, and said to him, Behold, thou *art but* a dead man, for the woman which thou hast taken; for she *is* a man's wife.

If Abimelech chose to ignore the dream, the consequences would be very serious; he would die!

Genesis 31:24 And God came to Laban the Syrian in a dream by night, and said unto him, Take heed that thou speak not to Jacob either good or bad.

God told Laban, the Syrian, not to speak bad words (threatening, demeaning) to Jacob. However, he was also warning Laban not to speak good words—sweet talk — trying to persuade Jacob to stay with him longer. Laban had tricked Jacob into staying in the past as payment for marriage to his daughters. God's purpose required Jacob to return to the Promised Land as directed in another dream. Laban was not to interfere with those plans. When he did meet up with Jacob, Laban obeyed what God told him in the dream. Jacob and the wellbeing of the nation were preserved because of that warning dream.

Matthew 2:12 And being warned of God in a dream that they should not return to Herod, they departed into their own country another way.

They obeyed the warning and Herod did not have immediate access to God's very own son.

Encouragement Dreams

Sometimes God uses dreams to show us where we are and to encourage us. These dreams motivate us to continue with the things of God.

Years ago God gave me a dream where many of my current team members (in Ministry) were all in front of this huge golden doors. There were two doors that we were all standing before. We opened the great golden doors and inside were the most beautiful site I ever saw. On our right and on our left were many treasure chests running over with jewelry, gemstones, gold and even scrolls. We all began to walk toward the most brilliant light and I began to see the most enormous feet with sandals on and then I saw a throne that He was sitting on. He spoke out to me and said there is room enough for all of you come!

After that dream we began to breakout in signs and wonders (treasure chests running over with jewelry, gemstones, gold) and the revelations (scrolls) began to flow like never before.

Guidance Dreams

Guidance dreams are those that give guidance or direction into the life of the dreamer.

Acts 16:9, 10 And a vision appeared to Paul in the night; There stood a man of Macedonia, and prayed him, saying, Come over into Macedonia, and help us. And after he had seen the vision, immediately we endeavoured to go into Macedonia, assuredly gathering that the Lord had called us for to preach the gospel unto them.

God spoke to Paul through this vision about a change in plans or a change in direction and Paul responded immediately by arranging a missionary venture into Macedonia.

The Lord knows how we struggle wanting to follow him without knowing where to go. Dreams can be a source of guidance.

Matthew 2:13, 14 And when they were departed, behold, the angel of the Lord appeareth to Joseph in a dream, saying, Arise, and take the young child and his mother, and flee into Egypt, and be thou there until I bring thee word: for Herod will seek the young child to destroy him. When he arose, he took the young child and his mother by night, and departed into Egypt:

God told Joseph to take Mary and Jesus to Egypt and, because Joseph obeyed, the life of God's own son was spared. The dream also told Joseph to remain in Egypt until God gave him further direction.

Revealing Dreams

The Lord gives dreams that reveal something not known or a future event. Sometimes these revelatory dreams are for the person themselves (subjective) and sometimes they speak of one's family, church, city, or the world (objective).

Warfare Dreams

Some warfare dreams come from the Lord to expose the plans of our spiritual enemy. I believe some plan of the enemy for our lives is revealed through dreams. Knowing in advance allowed us to pray and prevent whatever the enemy had planned.

Warfare dreams can involve the dreamer or others. These dreams may show descriptions such as an enemy trying to take our life, shooting at us, stalking us, trying to hurt us, or threatening our lives. There can also be feelings of great fear. These dreams may confirm the hatred of the enemy toward us.

We often wrongly label them as "nightmares," but they should be given attention. As children of God, we have a very real enemy who hates God but can do nothing to him. He targets the children of God. God, in these dreams, shows us the strategies of the enemy so we can prepare and defeat him.

Creativity Dreams

Many people receive creative inspiration through dreams. Our God has given some people new ideas for inventions, and musicians often receive lyrics or tunes that swirl in their minds in the night.

In the morning, the dreams yield great fruit. Scientists have been known to receive dreams with important information that led to cures. We have a most creative God. Dreams are one way he shares his creative nature with us.

Healing Dreams

This is an exciting and relatively new area within the ministry of inner healing. This inner healing, as it is often called, is an effective tool for bringing change and healing to relationships within the Church.

Unfortunately, much of the body is not yet aware of its need or of the existence of this opportunity. The principle behind inner healing is the person of Jesus. In prayer, we invite Jesus into the memories of our youth. There, He dispels the misunderstandings and lies believed about ourselves by the immature minds of our childhoods. As well, we come face to face with times we have broken one or more of God's spiritual laws during those early years.

We are then able to receive forgiveness, cleansing, and restoration through repentance and confession. Jesus has also shown himself to be well able to reach into the generational sins that plague many of us and there break the cycles that affect our lives today. Jesus is the only one who rightfully owns the title "Wonderful Counselor", and he truly is! I have witnessed this fact many times.

In the inner healing process, we act as facilitators to his work. This is sometimes easy and sometimes quite demanding. We are excited about the new things God is doing with dreams in the healing of memories. As we learn, through practice, to differentiate between message and miscellaneous dreams and then identify the purpose of the message dream, we are ready for the next step— working with the language of signs and images. That language deserves to be learned and understood so it can be the precious gift to us it is.

When Jesus first spoke to people in parables, the disciples were curious to know what he was saying through those stories. As we will learn in this, Jesus gave them keys to help get started. Those same principles help us in understanding the language of dreams, as we will see.

Some Basics

You should be careful not to make any meaning to dreams absolute. We must allow the Holy Spirit to adjust the meaning as we may go through the process. There almost seems to be a good and an evil meaning to images. Evaluate each meaning using details from the dream such as the color of the symbol, the posture, the eyes, the size, and especially the emotions you felt during the dream. These all hold a key to understanding the symbols. Give attention to the age of symbols, such as the home of your youth versus your present home. This is important, especially in healing, because it helps to identify the timing of the message. Many symbols can have biblical and a variety of personal meanings. Which meaning do you choose? Searching for God's message in your dream requires you to be very honest with yourself. We might choose to believe one meaning over another because one is more favorable.

However, doing so will rob us of the truth and of the benefits of the message. We believe there will be a witness in our spirit when we have the correct meaning and a gnawing feeling if we draw the wrong meaning. This, too, is part of the process of growing into an understanding of our dream language.

Please be careful with symbols. I ask you to consider them as stepping stones to building your own understanding of the message.

People

I believe people in subjective dreams can represent what they are in relationship to us or what their character represents to us.

It is also important to pay attention to the roles and names of people in your dreams, especially if the name is spoken. People's names have meaning and may be important to the dream.

I don't want to provide symbols much because I believe strongly in the personal approach to dream symbols. Providing any list creates opportunity to misuse the information. You will, over time, develop your own personal dictionary of dream symbols with meanings that will likely differ. God speaks to you different that He speaks to me.

The last issue of importance in understanding the dream, especially subjective dreams, involves context. When you dream, make a note of the context—the events in your life at the time of the dream—because a big part of the equation in the full understanding of your dreams is the matter of context. It is in the context of our lives at the time of the dream that the symbols begin to make sense and lead to understanding.

Chapter Nine
God Is Doing a New Thing

God has for years been speaking that He is going to do a new thing. We are in that time now. These days more than ever we need to pray for a depth of understanding regarding the purposes of God. We need the cobwebs of our mind swept away by the Spirit of God.

The Church must be realigned with God's present purpose and break out of the things that have made us irrelevant in this day and time. We are in transition now whether we like it or not—indeed, we are in a process of change whether we want it or want to avoid it! All change begins in the heart of God and makes its presence felt in our lives by His hand. There are times and seasons when God intervenes sovereignly in humanity to bring an end to one thing and a beginning to another.

Isaiah 42:9 Behold, the former things are come to pass, and new things do I declare: before they spring forth I tell you of them.

Isaiah 43:18, 19 Remember ye not the former things, neither consider the things of old. Behold, I will do a new thing; now it shall spring forth; shall ye not know it? I will even make a way in the wilderness, *and* rivers in the desert.

One of the characteristics of an outstanding leader is to know when change is imminent, to know the proclamations and declarations of the Spirit with regard to new times and fresh seasons.

Happy is the church that has such an understanding of the ways of the Lord! God has a dream about Church, and Jesus birthed that dream in the hearts of men. People under the influence of the Holy Spirit wrote concerning the dream in all its many forms. The Holy Spirit is given as our tutor and comes alongside as a friend to impart the dream and make it live within us.

What is this dream? It is that God would have a dwelling place amongst us...that the people, who make up the Church, would see themselves as living stones and allow themselves to be fitted and framed together in relationship and ministry...that God would inhabit our friendships to such a remarkable extent that His manifest presence would break out amongst all people groups everywhere.

Instead, we observe a Church fat with truth but impractical in revelation. We see an organization claiming biblical structure but manifesting a hierarchy world system of government. We have been falling away from God's new structure. Leaders are bent on titles, status, and position; ignoring servanthood, sacrifice, example, and stewardship. We have churches where we enjoy worship but have not learned corporately how to minister to the Lord...assemblies where we exalt the power of God but do little to attract His presence.

All around us are camps where we revere what God has said but have no clue as to what He is saying today. God used to speak, but since He has written a book, He lost His voice. In order to receive everything they need, some people have turned faith into an object of desire in itself. We only are willing to accept part of all that God wants to do.

To some, spiritual warfare is a myth, a work of fiction. To others, the focus on the demonic and the power of satan has relegated the majesty of Jesus to a place of seeming worthless.

Of course, the other side of this coin is quite different. Millions of people have faithfully stood their ground against dark opposition. Hundreds of thousands are being born again weekly throughout the earth. Countless numbers of churches have been renewed into a fresh awakening of God's love, mercy, and joy.

God is fulfilling His dream for the Church

There are abundant signs in every nation of the desire of God to break out in a fresh way to all people. Here we have the paradox of the modern-day Church.

(A paradox is the tension between two extremes.) The Church is a contradiction that can no longer be tolerated by Almighty God. We are being caught up into a new dimension of Kingdom activity that will jar us out of our complacency. The universal Church is in a state of profound change. There is a shaking taking place as God moves through His Body. New alignments are taking place, new relationships are forming, and current friendships are re-forming in a higher spiritual dimension and purpose.

There is an ongoing tactical shake-up taking place as God's new strategy for worldwide harvest comes off the drawing board and into our hearts for these last days. It is clear that the Lord is doing a new thing: He is presenting the Church with more new wineskins.

If the harvest did come right now all they would do is get poisoned by many of the lukewarm Churches.

The cutting edge of the Church has been moved forward into a new dimension where even the most forward-thinking and progressive churches will need to rethink their strategies for this new season of Holy Spirit activity. Whatever we think we understand, and have experienced about Church has probably not prepared us for all that God will be doing in this next phase.

He is doing a new thing! We must position ourselves where we can hear and bear all that the Lord wants to make known. Even Jesus said to His disciples at one point,

John 16:12 I have yet many things to say unto you, but ye cannot bear them now.

The Church is in a Season of Profound of Change

Revelation is not just centered on our ability to hear the Lord properly and receive progressive truth. It is also about our capacity to carry that truth and to be built into the new thing the Lord is creating. Revelation challenges our capacity to become what God is making. It is about bearing the weight of new responsibility, fresh anointing, and significant change. A prototype church must bear the weight of new revelation, new expectations, and new opposition if it is to become the prophetic model to fulfill God's end-time purpose. To create this Church, God has to speak "deep unto deep" in our spirit. This is not just about receiving some tactical information or prophetic insight into the next phase of church growth or ministry. It is about being instead of doing. It is not about the work of the ministry; it is about the image of Christ.

We have gone as far as we can go regarding revelation about the work of the church, strategies for reaching the harvest, and the development of gifts and workers. We have hit the ceiling of revelatory insight and cannot press through without a radical change of heart. The weight of revelation and Holy Spirit formation for this next phase will fall only on humble hearts that have a passion for Jesus Himself.

We are poised to enter a whole new spiritual dimension, a climate so thick with the presence of God that it will affect our ability to stand, let alone walk. We must bear a new imprint of the likeness of Christ. Jesus came to put a face on God.

Jesus was one man who was the full measure of God and we are to be the new representatives of Heaven. Jesus died and arose again for us to be able to have all that was lost in the Garden of Eden.

John 14:9 Jesus saith unto him, Have I been so long time with you, and yet hast thou not known me, Philip? he that hath seen me hath seen the Father; and how sayest thou *then,* Shew us the Father?

Building a Prototype Church

The Church is here to put a face on Christ. Renewal has given the Church something of a makeover in our spiritual personality. God is intent on giving us a face-lift to change our image.

In recent times, we have measured our success in church by numbers, budget increases, staff members, overseas missions, and the size and scope of varying projects. The only measure that will be acceptable in the next time frame is how much of the glory of God is contained in our meetings. God is restoring His manifest presence among us.

When the Lord says, "new," He means exactly that: new! When He declares an end to one thing and the beginning of a new order, He is dead serious.

To reinforce the concept, He orders His people to not be concerned or even think about the old thing ever again because He wants their attention to be on what He will do next!

Isaiah 43:19 Behold, **I will do a new thing**; now it shall spring forth; shall ye not know it? I will even make a way in the wilderness, *and* rivers in the desert.

Here we have a proclamation and question joined together, signifying intent. "I'm doing this, do you want to see?" The implication is that we must let go of the old in order to even see the new. There has to be a transformation in our thinking.

The Lord has drawn a line in Heaven. On one side are the former things—strategies, programs, ideas, and structures that once worked but are being discarded. They may still be effective, but now they are not required. The biggest danger to a new move of God is the last move that is still working! God wants to do a new thing. On the other side of the line will come revelation, anointing, and a fresh force of the Word and Spirit? His plans are set into a new dimension of activity within Heaven. He has new purpose. His hand is holding out new things to us. At that precise point, God obeys His own word. He turns His back on the old things and begins to look and speak into the new thing. The three most maligned people groups in the Church— prophetic people, intercessors, and worshipers—will immediately cross that line to stand under the smile of God. They have to be where God is looking at and speaking into. They move their feet in obedience to the heart of God. Ongoing revelation is positional. We have to move in obedience to the word of God. As we move, we progress into a place where we can hear and understand the next thing that God is communicating. If we fail to move, then our capacity to understand what God is saying and doing is diminished. Staying on the side of the line with the "former" things will put us at a disadvantage in receiving the new things that God is releasing. When we stay on the former side, words that come to us from the new side often do not compute with our thinking. Conceptually we can agree that change is needed and even desired.

Many have heard about the new things and reject them based on their old mind-set. If we fail to reposition ourselves before the Lord, we will water down the challenge of the new word to make it compatible with what we have already received in times past. We will own more allegiance to the former thing than commitment to the new process of God.

We need a willingness to move in obedience and a desire to be in the presence of God that is greater than our need for personal or corporate security.

As we know, most problems in churches occur because people will not move. People crossing the line come into revelation and a new level of anointing to implement truth. Some people who have stayed in place—which are now on the wrong side of God—cannot understand the new thing.

It's the same with progressive truth. You have to be in the place where it fits, where it can be worked out, to understand it.

Renewal, when it hit various churches it did not fit in with what they were doing. Many leaders did not understand how to respond. "Where does it fit with what we already have?" was their question. It didn't fit. It was not supposed to fit. It was given to re-engineer the church into a new place in God. The very idea that God should do only what fits with what He has already done is absurd.

He has seldom worked that way. Much of Jesus' message was prefaced with, "You have heard it said, but now I say to you...."

His words brought a change to people's perception of God and His workings. He warned people in Luke 5:36-39 that new wine needs a new wineskin.

Luke 5:36-39 And he spake also a parable unto them; No man putteth a piece of a new garment upon an old; if otherwise, then both the new maketh a rent, and the piece that was *taken* out of the new agreeth not with the old. And no man putteth new wine into old bottles; else the new wine will burst the bottles, and be spilled, and the bottles shall perish. But new wine must be put into new bottles; and both are preserved. No man also having drunk old *wine* straightway desireth new: for he saith, The old is better.

It seems fairly amazing that the new wine of renewal should be rejected because it did not mix well with the old form of meetings that we were used to. Of course it meant change. God will not fit in with us. He helps us to adjust to Him.

Is the church for people or is it for God? Of course it is for both, but who has priority? Are the meetings too man-centered, revolving around ministering to people? Do we even know how to corporately minister to the Lord? Has our Church become so far removed from God's presence that His glory never falls? Sadly, our current experience of God seems more centered on His *omni-presence* than His *manifest* presence.

What has happened from the early days of the charismatic movement has continued till the present day in many places. Then as now, new wineskins had to form, many of them through splits of varying kinds. A new piece of cloth cannot be attached to an old garment without stretching it and causing it to tear. New moves play havoc with old moves unless we trade in what we have for what God wants to give us.

Transition is about trading in church, new for old. Many leaders do not cross the line to be where God is looking and speaking; therefore, their revelation becomes secondhand.

Often, people on one side of the line criticize the new thing. We always criticize what we don't understand. They reject it, neglect it, misinterpret it, and criticize it—until they see that it is working. Then they take hold of a mixture form; that is, they grab on to something that is a cut-down version that will fit their current model, and they bolt it on to what they already have.

Home groups, electronic music equipment, deliverance, the prophetic, contemporary worship, team ministry, youth church—these are merely a few. These all began life in criticism and dire warnings.

We bolt new things onto our existing structure of church, but the basic model remains the same. Our meetings are still the same style—just slightly longer, perhaps. They are just as boring and noncreative, with the same people participating.

Many people seek a radical expression of church as an antidote to their current meetings. They push for a radical demonstration but do not achieve anything because the heart of their cry is not locked into a deep-seated dependency upon God Himself. The pursuit of cultural relevance and trendy ways of exhibiting the gospel will be just as impotent and people-consuming as any other method. We want the fullness of God. Only His presence is relevant to every issue.

Only He can touch people and bring radical change. If, through you, God can heal sick bodies, renew people's minds, restore dignity through salvation, deliver people of demons, and present the fullness of His presence, then you are culturally relevant!

We still have this unbiblical void between clergy and laity. Many believers are still treated as pew food every week. They are fed one-man ministry, irrelevant sermons, and little supernatural expression, experience, or expectation. Many Christians do not have a personal vision to serve God, are not being discipled or empowered, and have no idea of where they fit into local church and the wider Kingdom of Heaven.

If we do not move our feet, we can only adapt to the will of God—not be changed by it. Even in the midst of God's moving today, we are trying to maintain business as usual. We talk about brokenness but seldom allow the presence of God to break in.

We yearn to be radical but don't recognize the sharpening that comes from a cutting edge move of God. Are we being renewed or is it business as usual? It seems that both do not always connect together.

If our current mind-set does not allow us to experience the will of God, then it is time to change our thinking. Are we really prepared to change our ideas about church? What are those ideas based on and shaped by?

This will not be a painless transition. There will be people who disagree when you move forward. There always is religion fighting the new things. People who leave Churches during a transition were never really a part.

CHAPTER TEN
Does God Share Your Theology?

I want you to really realize that we are continually being exposed to more supernatural and more revelations. An idea shapes the way we think, forming an ideology. This, in turn, can affect our theology, or what we see and understand in Scripture. Our theology can be made to fit our ideas of how things should be.

Matthew 20:1-16 For the kingdom of heaven is like unto a man *that is* an householder, which went out early in the morning to hire labourers into his vineyard. And when he had agreed with the labourers for a penny a day, he sent them into his vineyard. And he went out about the third hour, and saw others standing idle in the marketplace, And said unto them; Go ye also into the vineyard, and whatsoever is right I will give you. And they went their way. Again he went out about the sixth and ninth hour, and did likewise. And about the eleventh hour he went out, and found others standing idle, and saith unto them, Why stand ye here all the day idle? They say unto him, Because no man hath hired us. He saith unto them, Go ye also into the vineyard; and whatsoever is right, *that* shall ye receive. So when even was come, the lord of the vineyard saith unto his steward, Call the labourers, and give them *their* hire, beginning from the last unto the first. And when they came that *were hired* about the eleventh hour, they received every man a penny. But when the first came, they supposed that they should have received more; and they likewise received every man a penny. And when they had received *it,* they murmured against the goodman of the house, Saying, These last have wrought *but* one hour, and thou hast made them equal unto us, which have borne the burden and heat of the day. But he answered one of them, and said, Friend, I do thee no wrong: didst not thou agree with me for a penny? Take *that* thine *is,* and go thy way: I will give unto this last, even as unto thee. Is it not lawful for me to do what I will with mine own? Is thine eye evil, because I am good? So the last shall be first, and the first last: for many be called, but few chosen.

Let's reflect on this story: The landowner, throughout the day, hired laborers to work in his vineyard. He paid them all the same wage, regardless of how many hours they worked. When those who worked all day saw this, they protested.

The landowner replied, "I am not doing anything wrong; you agreed to work for this amount. It's my choice to be generous to the others".

The theology in this parable is this: God has the perfect right to do whatever He wishes with His substance and His people. Because the first laborers did not understand this, they felt insulted and not blessed by the landowner's generosity. Their idea was that those who work harder and longer should receive more payment.

This is perfectly sound, but on this occasion it does not fit with God's viewpoint or intended practice. Their theology was rooted in their own ideology about what is fair and just. They were unhappy and disturbed by their own perception of how things should work. Jesus' point was that people's understanding of God should conform to who He really is and how He wants to conduct Himself!

An idea of how things should be becomes an idea when we attempt to surround it with ethics and morality. On top of that ideology we construct a theology. We try to connect a number of Scriptures to how we feel about things. In this way the Scriptures become a proof text for what we feel ought to be the truth. This is not enough for some people who take it a step further in their thinking. Drawing from a number of sources, the marriage of ideology and theology produces a philosophy that is rooted in a mental concept of God and human faith, not a spiritual context.

Their thinking is rooted in a ghostly twilight zone suspended between the natural and the spiritual realms. It is soulish and full of mental and emotional terminology.

Philosophy requires psychology to keep it in place. The study of human behavior is needed to enable people to express their views in acceptable form as well as to control how those views are received. When we meet resistance, we can make our response according to our perception of the intellectual and educational capacity of the individual concerned. If that person has no access to primary education at the highest level, he may be deemed naïve and simplistic. Should the opposite be true, we possibly surmise that *he* may have opinions and ideas not rooted in the real world of practical day-to-day living.

The point I wish to make is this: How often is this jumble of ideology, theology, philosophy, and psychology put together and used on the people of God? Examine the whole principle of one-man ministry in the church.

We must understand the full picture.

A brief look at the Scriptures tells us that the term *pastor* is not a descriptive word for a local church leader. It is used only once in connection with the fivefold ministries of apostle, prophet, pastor, teacher, and evangelist.

The correct term for local leadership is the plural of *elder* to denote a team ministry. Pastors are considered elders according to scriptures.

Acts 11:30 Which also they did, and sent it to the **elders** by the hands of Barnabas and Saul.

Acts 14:23 And when they had ordained them **elders** in every church, and had prayed with fasting, they commended them to the Lord, on whom they believed.

Acts 15:2 When therefore Paul and Barnabas had no small dissension and disputation with them, they determined that Paul and Barnabas, and certain other of them, should go up to Jerusalem unto the **apostles and elders** about this question.

Acts 15:4 And when they were come to Jerusalem, they were received of the church, and *of* the **apostles and elders**, and they declared all things that God had done with them.

Acts 15:6 And the **apostles and elders** came together for to consider of this matter.

Acts 15:22 Then pleased it the **apostles and elders**, with the whole church, to send chosen men of their own company to Antioch with Paul and Barnabas; *namely,* Judas surnamed Barsabas, and Silas, chief men among the brethren:

Acts 16:4 And as they went through the cities, they delivered them the decrees for to keep, that were ordained of the **apostles and elders** which were at Jerusalem.

Acts 20:17 And from Miletus he sent to Ephesus, and called the **elders** of the church.

Acts 20:28 Take heed therefore unto yourselves, and to all the flock, over the which the Holy Ghost hath made you overseers, to feed the church of God, which he hath purchased with his own blood.

Acts 21:18 And the *day* following Paul went in with us unto James; and all the **elders** were present.

1Timothy 3:1-7 This *is* a true saying, If a man desire the office of a bishop, he desireth a good work. A bishop then must be blameless, the husband of one wife, vigilant, sober, of good behaviour, given to hospitality, apt to teach; Not given to wine, no striker, not greedy of filthy lucre; but patient, not a brawler, not covetous; One that ruleth well his own house, having his children in subjection with all gravity; (For if a man know not how to rule his own house, how shall he take care of the church of God?) Not a novice, lest being lifted up with pride he fall into the condemnation of the devil. Moreover he must have a good report of them which are without; lest he fall into reproach and the snare of the devil.

1Timothy 5:17 Let the **elders** that rule well be counted worthy of double honour, especially they who labour in the word and doctrine.

Titus 1:5-9 For this cause left I thee in Crete, that thou shouldest set in order the things that are wanting, and ordain **elders** in every city, as I had appointed thee: If any be blameless, the husband of one wife, having faithful children not accused of riot or unruly. For a bishop must be blameless, as the steward of God; not selfwilled, not soon angry, not given to wine, no striker, not given to filthy lucre; But a lover of hospitality, a lover of good men, sober, just, holy, temperate; Holding fast the faithful word as he hath been taught, that he may be able by sound doctrine both to exhort and to convince the gainsayers.

James 5:14 Is any sick among you? let him call for the **elders** of the church; and let them pray over him, anointing him with oil in the name of the Lord:

1Peter 5:1-4 The elders which are among you I exhort, who am also an **elder**, and a witness of the sufferings of Christ, and also a partaker of the glory that shall be revealed: Feed the flock of God which is among you, taking the oversight *thereof,* not by constraint, but willingly; not for filthy lucre, but of a ready mind; Neither as being lords over *God's* heritage, but being ensamples to the flock. And when the chief Shepherd shall appear, ye shall receive a crown of glory that fadeth not away.

Elders have more of an active role in the Church according to scriptures. Elders are a group of dedicated people working together in love and friendship to produce men and women with anointed lifestyles and ministries to empower the work of God in the locality and further afield. In all the New Testament churches established under apostolic and prophetic input we read of elders (plural) being appointed in every city.

Acts 14:23 And when they had ordained them elders in every church, and had prayed with fasting, they commended them to the Lord, on whom they believed.

Building a Prototype Church

The apostolic team working through and in support of local teams of elders would train, equip, empower, and release the people to do the work of the ministry. The fivefold ministries are mentor gifts to church leaders (and often are leaders in churches themselves) to enable them to be built wisely into the place of anointed significance that God desires for them in that locality. Many pastors today may not like this revelation. They may be concerned about their salary or position. If we all line up, God will provide for all of us.

When I was a Pastor of a Church in 2005 many told me it would fail. I was operating in the office of a Prophet and they would say "you have to be in the office of a Pastor to succeed. I was there for five years and when my season ended there the Church was packed with miracles, signs and wonders happening in every service. Apostles and Prophets are a vital part of the foundation and leadership of the Church. If not in place there will be instability.

What we have in thousands of churches today is a one-man ministry approach that cannot be defended in Scripture. The principle for this philosophy was set several of years ago and follows this thought process: Only learned and intelligent people can rule in the church because most of the people are uneducated and illiterate.

There is obviously a place for intelligent and intellectual ability within the church. Most of charismatic Christianity has kissed its brains good-bye in the search for spiritual experience.

Is your church an audience or an army?

Much of what passes for Christianity is dry, ritualistic, and intellectual. In actual fact, the early Church fathers were a fascinating mix of the intelligent and the illiterate.

Acts 26:24 And as he thus spake for himself, Festus said with a loud voice, Paul, thou art beside thyself; much learning doth make thee mad.

The Church is in a Season of Profound of Change

After the religious leaders had questioned them and listened closely to Peter and John's answers, they made several observations.

Acts 4:1-14 And as they spake unto the people, the priests, and the captain of the temple, and the Sadducees, came upon them, Being grieved that they taught the people, and preached through Jesus the resurrection from the dead. And they laid hands on them, and put *them* in hold unto the next day: for it was now eventide. Howbeit many of them which heard the word believed; and the number of the men was about five thousand. And it came to pass on the morrow, that their rulers, and elders, and scribes, And Annas the high priest, and Caiaphas, and John, and Alexander, and as many as were of the kindred of the high priest, were gathered together at Jerusalem. And when they had set them in the midst, they asked, By what power, or by what name, have ye done this? Then Peter, filled with the Holy Ghost, said unto them, Ye rulers of the people, and elders of Israel, If we this day be examined of the good deed done to the impotent man, by what means he is made whole; Be it known unto you all, and to all the people of Israel, that by the name of Jesus Christ of Nazareth, whom ye crucified, whom God raised from the dead, *even* by him doth this man stand here before you whole. This is the stone which was set at nought of you builders, which is become the head of the corner. Neither is there salvation in any other: for there is none other name under heaven given among men, whereby we must be saved. Now when they saw the boldness of Peter and John, and perceived that they were unlearned and ignorant men, they marvelled; and they took knowledge of them, that they had been with Jesus. And beholding the man which was healed standing with them, they could say nothing against it.

1. Peter and John were extremely confident in God and what they were doing.
2. They were unlearned and ignorant.
3. Peter and John had spent time with Jesus.

The early apostles, then, were a team of extremes—educated and refined like Paul and Luke but also illiterate fishermen like Peter, James, and John—and probably several shades in-between.

In today's church culture, Peter and John's lack of formal training would make them eligible only for the laity, yet they were apostles!

Real theology does not come from books or schools. It arises out of repentant hearts, submissive spirits, and renewed minds. Real theology is spoken in the language of slaves and ignorant fishermen. It is based on time spent with Jesus and the confidence that His presence engenders in human hearts. It has learning and experience. It is both taught by men and distilled in relationship with the Holy Spirit. Real theology is not meant only for arguing points but also for creatively demonstrating the nature and character of God through both His words and His works.

Theology and experience combine to train the people of God to do the ministry. So much of what is learned in Bible College and seminary is useless in the process of building the church to fulfill the dreams of God.

The two most powerful questions we can ask today are "What?" and "Why?" "What are we doing, and why are we doing it?" We must have a mind-set and a theology that proves the will of God and helps us to build the Kingdom. "Is what we are doing still working? Is it effective? Can it work better? How do we change it? What is God saying to us this year?"

Much leadership does not build in time for review, prayer, and corporate examination of the vision, anointing, and ministry of their church. Are we merely bolting what works on to our existing structures that don't work? We have to let go of old to claim the new things. Is the life of the church serving the structure and the program, or is the program and structure producing life and faith in relationship and service to the Lord? A revolution in leadership is required to bring us back into alignment with the early Church.

With all of our Western style of leadership we have created a church that consumes rather than a church that produces. We have generated an audience, not an army....people who do hear but who does not live out the Word.

We are seeing a shift from not being hearers only but also being doers.

Chapter Eleven
Paradigm Shift

We need a paradigm shift in our thinking. This shift must take place to proceed toward the Prototype Church. A *paradigm* is a new level of thinking. Most paradigm shifts begin in the prophetic, because its roots are in the heart of God. A paradigm shift occurs when our new minds radically affect our behavior and the way that we operate. The problem is people are thinking about new paradigms, or new concepts, but their behavior still hasn't changed. They are still trying to bolt the new things onto the old things that they have always done. We have to turn our back on what the Lord deems to be old and press into what He is opening up before us. Former things and new things almost always relate to structure, methodology, operation of church, and practice of ministry.

The Bible does not say too much about meetings.

Hebrews 10:25 **Not forsaking the assembling of ourselves together**, as the manner of some *is;* but exhorting *one another:* and so much the more, as ye see the day approaching.

The Bible really only says that we are to meet together. The other half simply talks about creativity and the possibility that our meetings, when led by the Spirit, have the capacity to be different on every occasion.

1Corinthians 14:6 Now, brethren, if I come unto you speaking with tongues, what shall I profit you, except I shall speak to you either by revelation, or by knowledge, or by prophesying, or by doctrine?

God does not give specific details on how, when, or how often to meet. He knows that if He gave us specific details, we would use them to set the whole thing in concrete forever! We have developed a style full of rigid ways and stereotype even with the bare information He gave us. When we meet on Sundays almost every Church meets at the same time. Just think of the mess we would have created with more detailed instructions. If God is vague or indefinite about anything, it is always for a specific reason.

In this case, His lack of definition was intended to keep us as close to Him as possible. He wants us to move by every word that comes out of His mouth. Lack of definition is intended to create a dependency upon God in us so that we will be led by Him as He desires.

Structure and operation are also concerned with:

1. How we conduct the ministry of the church outside our own meetings.
2. How we disciple and prepare people for works of service.
3. Our mission to the nation and the nations.
4. The vision and calling of the church.
5. The development and release of the next generation of leaders and ministries.
6. How we conduct ourselves in worship, prayer, spiritual warfare, financial giving, and work amongst the poor.
7. Our relationship and unity with other churches in the area.
8. Our understanding and practice of the gospel of the Kingdom.

All of these things can be touched, changed, and redirected by the Lord as He sees fit. When He speaks into those things, His words create a paradigm shift in our hearts.

The word *paradigm* is derived from the Greek word *paradeigma*, meaning "pattern." A pattern is a model or a guide used for making something.

A paradigm relates to the set of beliefs usually concealed in the code of behavior with which we interpret events surrounding our life. We have paradigms that govern how we see ourselves, our church, and our country in relation to the world around us.

Everyone said that a plane would never fly but today millions of people are flying all over the world. When a paradigm shifts, we see and understand new information, but the very way we see and understand is also changed.

When we experience a true paradigm shift, everything goes back to zero. God doesn't build the next thing out of the old thing. The old passes away; the new thing arrives. We need a revelation to know what the new thing is and how it works. We must go back to the drawing board and be prepared to lay everything down. This is the zero perspective. Everything belongs to God, so lay it on the altar. The promise and vision of all that God has, is, and will give us, must always be submitted to a potential death. It is His, not ours.

Like Abraham, we take to our hearts that which is God given and precious beyond the telling, and we offer it up to the Lord. Is this a pretend offering because we expect God to refuse it? No. We raise the knife with only an expectancy that He will still provide for us—if not this son, then another one.

Genesis 22:1-12 And it came to pass after these things, that God did tempt Abraham, and said unto him, Abraham: and he said, Behold, *here* I *am*. And he said, Take now thy son, thine only *son* Isaac, whom thou lovest, and get thee into the land of Moriah; and offer him there for a burnt offering upon one of the mountains which I will tell thee of. And Abraham rose up early in the morning, and saddled his ass, and took two of his young men with him, and Isaac his son, and clave the wood for the burnt offering, and rose up, and went unto the place of which God had told him. Then on the third day Abraham lifted up his eyes, and saw the place afar off. And Abraham said unto his young men, Abide ye here with the ass; and I and the lad will go yonder and worship, and come again to you. And Abraham took the wood of the burnt offering, and laid *it* upon Isaac his son; and he took the fire in his hand, and a knife; and they went both of them together. And Isaac spake unto Abraham his father, and said, My father: and he said, Here *am* I, my son. And he said, Behold the fire and the wood: but where *is* the lamb for a burnt offering? And Abraham said, My son, God will provide himself a lamb for a burnt offering: so they went both of them together. And they came to the place which God had told him of; and Abraham built an altar there, and laid the wood in order, and bound Isaac his son, and laid him on the altar upon the wood. And Abraham stretched forth his hand, and took the knife to slay his son. And the angel of the LORD called unto him out of heaven, and said, Abraham, Abraham: and he said, Here *am* I. And he said, Lay not thine hand upon the lad, neither do thou any thing unto him: for now I know that thou fearest God, seeing thou hast not withheld thy son, thine only *son* from me.

If the Lord returns it to you, it may be taken up and used. It may return reshaped and different. The period between the old being laid down and the new being put into place is called *transition*. Some of the old things will change and be reshaped, and new things will be added. The principal idea is that we should be unrecognizable in operation and methodology at the same time as retaining our integrity and character. The nature of the church remains the same, but the operational model of the church is rebuilt as we learn to occupy a new level of revelation and practice. God never changes in personality, but everything around Him changes in practice. We are constantly being made over in the image of Christ at the same time as God has His perfect will in our ministry. Transition is about the church maintaining the nature and character of God as He redevelops its role and operation to suit the next dimension of power He is bestowing upon us. Transition is about tension, change, uncertainty, fear, disturbance, redirection, remodeling, mess, excitement, re-envisioning, new call, fresh faith, unpredictability, frustration, disagreement, adventure, moving on, uprooting and the unknown!

All these things will test our capacity to express the nature of God in the fruit of the Spirit. Spirit versus carnality is a major part of transition. Basically, if the Spirit wins, we move on successfully in a remodeled church with a new anointing, fresh faith, and a new sense of mission and destiny. No matter who you are there are transitions ahead of you. If the flesh wins, our carnality will split the church.

CHAPTER TWELVE
Servant Leaders

Servants and Leaders are to be one and the same. Today Leaders have less servanthood than ever before. In times of transition, the scope of anointing and vision in our leadership changes dramatically. Some are marked for new vision and a fresh leadership empowerment.

The problem comes when we think of leadership as a title, status, or position. It is none of these things. Leadership is a function. The particular term used to define it relates to the job description of the activity involved. To put the title of Apostle, Prophet, Pastor, Bishop, etc. in front of our name is ludicrous and silly. Jesus never did. The apostles all called themselves apostles *and* bond slaves, signifying that both were equal terms that defined their role and job description. If they were meant to be used as titles, they would rightly cancel each other out. Paul referred to apostles as the scum of the earth.

1Corinthians 4:9-13 For I think that God hath set forth us the apostles last, as it were appointed to death: for we are made a spectacle unto the world, and to angels, and to men. We *are* fools for Christ's sake, but ye *are* wise in Christ; we *are* weak, but ye *are* strong; ye *are* honourable, but we *are* despised. Even unto this present hour we both hunger, and thirst, and are naked, and are buffeted, and have no certain dwellingplace; And labour, working with our own hands: being reviled, we bless; being persecuted, we suffer it: Being defamed, we intreat: we are made as the filth of the world, *and are* the offscouring of all things unto this day.

He referred to apostles as men condemned to death; a spectacle; an exhibit no one wants to see; fools; weak; without honor; destitute; reviled; persecuted; scum; and the remains of all things. Which of those things is a title? I always refer to my ministry as the very bottom of everything. Apostles and Prophets are the foundation to the Body of Christ. They all belong to God's apostleship and bond slavery. If we view these things as titles, as markers of status and position, we will tend to cling to the office that we feel is ours. This creates rival factions if people are defending their position.

There is nothing more unwholesome and ungodly in a church than to see people in positions of leadership holding on to power and position at any cost.

1Corinthians 11:1 Be ye followers of me, even as I also *am* of Christ.

Philippians 3:17 Brethren, be followers together of me, and mark them which walk so as ye have us for an ensample.

1Corinthians 4:16 Wherefore I beseech you, be ye followers of me.

Philippians 4:9 Those things, which ye have both learned, and received, and heard, and seen in me, do: and the God of peace shall be with you.

1Thessalonions 1:6 And ye became followers of us, and of the Lord, having received the word in much affliction, with joy of the Holy Ghost:

2Thessalonions 3:9 Not because we have not power, but to make ourselves an ensample unto you to follow us.

Paul constantly talked about the power of example and the need for good leadership models for the church to follow. Jesus Himself also talked about how those who desire to become leaders must be servants.

Mark 10:42-45 But Jesus called them *to him,* and saith unto them, Ye know that they which are accounted to rule over the Gentiles exercise lordship over them; and their great ones exercise authority upon them. But so shall it not be among you: but whosoever will be great among you, shall be your minister: And whosoever of you will be the chiefest, shall be servant of all. For even the Son of man came not to be ministered unto, but to minister, and to give his life a ransom for many.

There is an example in leadership that is grounded in servanthood, stewardship, and slavery—not in title, status, or position. There is no status in the Body of Christ. We are building church with Kingdom values, not with those of a hierarchic world system. Leaders are to be the best examples of servanthood and slavery in the church. It was the model set by Jesus and maintained by the apostles and leaders of the early Church.

Philippians 2:3-8 *Let* nothing *be done* through strife or vainglory; but in lowliness of mind let each esteem other better than themselves. Look not every man on his own things, but every man also on the things of others. Let this mind be in you, which was also in Christ Jesus: Who, being in the form of God, thought it not robbery to be equal with God: But made himself of no reputation, and took upon him the form of a servant, and was made in the likeness of men: And being found in fashion as a man, he humbled himself, and became obedient unto death, even the death of the cross.

If we are unable or unwilling to follow the model of our Lord and the apostle Paul, we should consider the image we are creating around ourselves. If it is not one of humility and servanthood, then we need to surrender ourselves. We need to be released from title, position, and status into servanthood, stewardship, and slavery.

On the other hand, we must be released from the ministry into secular employment where our poor attitude cannot have a negative impact on the church.

If we hold on to our position and status in times of tension and difficulty, we are liable to create a faction within the church. Paul said that the purpose of such factions would be to reveal who are the real leaders and who are the false. In times of tension and difficulty, those whom God approves become evident! We will know who is part of the Prototype Church by the evidence of their fruit.

1Corinthians 11:18, 19 For first of all, when ye come together in the church, I hear that there be divisions among you; and I partly believe it. For there must be also heresies among you, that they which are approved may be made manifest among you.

The church needs to become mature in identifying Christ-like behavior. Never be impressed by anointing. Only be joined to people who practice the fruit of the Spirit and not just the gifts. People can destroy with their character what they have built with their gift. Be rightly impressed by the nature, character, and image of Christ that is evident in people's lives. The Lord can add gifting relatively quickly, but character takes years of making righteous decisions in order to develop integrity.

The Church is in a Season of Profound of Change

Chapter Thirteen
Dunamis Power

The Prototype Churches will be full of God's Power. Two thousand years ago at God's set time, the fire and wind of God touched down in our world, right on the heads of about 120 believers--believers just like you and me. While they were gathered together with one heart, waiting upon the Lord Jesus after His death and resurrection, God decided it was the right moment to flip them all upside down and then stand them up again with a whole new DNA. They were never the same again!

Are you longing to experience a "happening" like that--an event that could potentially "rip you out" to rock the world with the Gospel of Jesus Christ?

Are you getting prepared in your heart for something like that?

We're living in revolutionary days!! The church is going to go out with a greater bang than it came in with! I believe what happened in the age of the New Testament--New Testament power, the birthing of the New Testament Church, and the early church--is only the beginning.

Haggai 2:7-9 And I will shake all nations, and the desire of all nations shall come: and I will fill this house with glory, saith the LORD of hosts. The silver *is* mine, and the gold *is* mine, saith the LORD of hosts. The glory of this latter house shall be greater than of the former, saith the LORD of hosts: and in this place will I give peace, saith the LORD of hosts.

I believe that God isn't going to come back until certain things happen in the church (all over the world). Before He comes again, He's going to release what we see in the beginning of the book of

Acts. It's going to look the same as it did in the New Testament church!

Acts 3:19-21 Repent ye therefore, and be converted, that your sins may be blotted out, when the times of refreshing shall come from the presence of the Lord; And he shall send Jesus Christ, which before was preached unto you: Whom the heaven must receive until the times of restitution of all things, which God hath spoken by the mouth of all his holy prophets since the world began.

The promise and the anointing are going to come back again. All things are going to be restored!

Hebrews 8:6 But now hath he obtained a more excellent ministry, by how much also he is the mediator of a better covenant, which was established upon better promises.

Exodus 13:21 And the LORD went before them by day in a pillar of a cloud, to lead them the way; and by night in a pillar of fire, to give them light; to go by day and night:

Exodus 14:21, 22 And Moses stretched out his hand over the sea; and the LORD caused the sea to go *back* by a strong east wind all that night, and made the sea dry *land,* and the waters were divided. And the children of Israel went into the midst of the sea upon the dry *ground:* and the waters *were* a wall unto them on their right hand, and on their left.

We're not yet walking in the streets and the market places in New Testament power with miracles, signs, and wonders. We're not living like they did in the Book of Acts yet.

However, God wants us to live like they did, to the point that the glory of the latter house is greater than the former. That's how the church will go out with a bigger bang than it came in with!

Yes, we have some exciting days to look forward to! I believe that God is restoring, and that He wants to open up the anointing that we're hungry for. He'll give us the same anointing that the apostles walked in, in the book of Acts. God wants us to realize that we'll be thrust forward or propelled into these momentous days by receiving and believing those same promises that He gave to the New Testament church. I say all this with even more assurance, now, because of a prophetic experience I had when the Lord spoke into my heart.

Acts 1:5 For John truly baptized with water; but ye shall be baptized with the Holy Ghost not many days hence.

What a promise from God! You shall be baptized with the Holy Spirit! Right now, the Lord is offering a fresh baptism of the Holy Spirit! Listen. I know some of you have already been baptized in the Holy Ghost, you are speaking in tongues, you've lived Pentecost. Maybe you've been in a Pentecostal Church for the last ten years. But I have a word that I want to declare to you today, that not many days from now, you shall be baptized with the Holy Ghost!

I believe we, the church in North America, have an opportunity to actually operate in the word of the Lord called "dunamis." Dunamis (Greek) means dynamic, great power, strength, force, capability; raw power to accomplish something.

Acts 1:8 But ye shall receive power, after that the Holy Ghost is come upon you: and ye shall be witnesses unto me both in Jerusalem, and in all Judaea, and in Samaria, and unto the uttermost part of the earth.

God wants to release dunamis power for miracles, signs, and wonders--resurrection power, raising the dead power--to be witnesses. That's the word of the Lord.

We're actually in a time when God wants to release a healing anointing, and miracles, signs, and wonders that will bring us to the harvest and to revival. Jesus healed great multitudes and when they came to Him to hear the word and get healed, many became believers. Today, God wants people to receive healing and then great multitudes will come and hear the word. That's where I believe we are prophetically. God's heart is for the lost! The Lord is saying for those of you that are hungry, not many days from now, you shall be baptized with the Holy Ghost.

When the Holy Ghost comes upon you, you're going to receive power to be God's witness in "Judea, Samaria, and the outermost parts of the earth." You're going to receive dunamis power. How did the disciples receive this empowerment? What did they do? They waited in the Upper Room!

Luke 24:49 And, behold, I send the promise of my Father upon you: but tarry ye in the city of Jerusalem, until ye be endued with power from on high.

God says, for those that will wait and tarry the way that the disciples waited and tarried in Jerusalem, I will give this prophetic promise of the endowment of My power.

Immediately the disciples were released into miracles, signs, and wonders! They received miracle-working dunamis power. Boldly they carried a demonstration of the power of God into their region and then to the uttermost parts of the earth. They said in their hearts that however long it takes they were going to be there, and they set a place, and they set a time, because they were so hungry. And get this! They were in one accord for ten days in that Upper Room. Ten days! In fact, "ten days" in that Upper Room really hit me. Our normal prayer life (a little prayer here and there) will not sustain us to be the history makers that God wants us to be.

Chapter Fourteen
God's Will For Healing

I used to believe "Lord if it be Your will I'll be healed. After a while I learned it is God's Will for all of us to be healed. One of the things we must understand is that we should be a new Church of healing. God has a will concerning healing. The most important thing in spiritual warfare is knowing what God's will is. It makes little difference what other people say about healing.

The question that must be asked is, "What did God say about it?" Before people can war for healing for themselves or for other people, they must be getting rid of all uncertainty concerning God's will in the matter.

Warring faith cannot go beyond our knowledge of what the revealed will of God is. We must know what the Scriptures plainly teach, that it is just as much God's will to heal the body as it is to heal the soul.

Until we know what God's will is, there is nothing to base our warring or our faith on. Praying for healing with the faith-destroying words, "If it be Thy will" is not warring. It is destroying the sick person. The prayer that will bring healing follows knowing the Word upon which alone faith is based.

Matthew 8:17 That it might be fulfilled which was spoken by Esaias the prophet, saying, Himself took our infirmities, and bare *our* sicknesses.

1Peters 2:24 Who his own self bare our sins in his own body on the tree, that we, being dead to sins, should live unto righteousness: by whose stripes ye were healed.

Healing and Salvation Go Hand in Hand throughout Scripture. To say *healed* or to say *saved* means the same thing. What the Godhead Says about Sickness God called sickness "captivity."

Job 42:10 And the LORD turned the captivity of Job, when he prayed for his friends: also the LORD gave Job twice as much as he had before.

Luke 13:16 And ought not this woman, being a daughter of Abraham, whom Satan hath bound, lo, these eighteen years, be loosed from this bond on the sabbath day?

Acts 10:38 How God anointed Jesus of Nazareth with the Holy Ghost and with power: who went about doing good, and healing all that were oppressed of the devil; for God was with him.

For a picture of the healing ministry of Jesus, carefully read the following accounts:

•• The healing of the man with the unclean spirit (see Mark 1:23; Luke 4:33).

•• The healing of Peter's mother-in-law (see Matthew 8:14; Mark 1:30; Luke 4:38).

•• The healing of multitudes (see Matthew 4:23; 8:16; 9:35; 11:4; 12:15; 14:14,34; 15:30; 19:2; Mark 1:32; 3:10; 6:55; Luke 4:40; 6:17; 7:21; 9:11; John 6:2).

•• The healing of the leper (see Matthew 8:2; Mark 1:40; Luke 5:12).

•• The healing of the man with palsy (see Matthew 9:2; Mark 2:3; Luke 5:17).

•• The healing of the man with the withered hand (see Matthew 12:9; Mark 3:1; Luke 6:6).

•• The healing of the demoniac of Gadara (see Matthew 8:28; Mark 5:1; Luke 8:26).

•• The healing of Jairus' daughter (see Matthew 9:18; Mark 5:22; Luke 8:41).

•• The healing of the woman with the issue of blood (see Matthew 9:20; Mark 5:25; Luke 8:43).

•• The healing of a few sick people (see Matthew 13:58; Mark 6:5).

•• The healing of the deaf and dumb man (see Mark 7:32).

•• The healing of the blind man (see Mark 8:22).

•• The healing of the child with an evil spirit (see Matthew 17:14; Mark 9:14; Luke 9:38).

•• The healing of blind Bartimaeus (see Matthew 20:30; Mark 10:46; Luke 18:35).

•• The healing of the centurian's servant (see Matthew 8:5; Luke 7:2).

•• The healing of two blind men (see Matthew 9:27).

•• The healing of the dumb demoniac (see Matthew 9:32).

•• The healing of the blind and dumb demoniac (see Matthew 12:22; Luke 11:14).

•• The healing of the blind and lame man in the temple (see Matthew 21:14).

•• The healing of the widow's son (see Luke 7:11).

•• The healing of Mary Magdalene and others (see Luke 8:2).

•• The healing of the woman bound by satan (see Luke 13:10).

•• The healing of the man with dropsy (see Luke 14:1).

•• The healing of the ten lepers (see Luke 17:11).

•• The healing of the nobleman's son (see John 4:46).

•• The healing of the impotent man (see John 5:5).

•• The healing of the man born blind (see John 9:1).

•• The healing of Lazarus (see John 11:1).

Christ used the same word to rebuke sickness and evil spirits.

Luke 4:35 And Jesus rebuked him, saying, Hold thy peace, and come out of him. And when the devil had thrown him in the midst, he came out of him, and hurt him not.

Christ used the same harsh word to rebuke all sicknesses as he used to rebuke all evil spirits, because all sickness is caused by Satan.

Acts 4:28-30 For to do whatsoever thy hand and thy counsel determined before to be done. And now, Lord, behold their threatenings: and grant unto thy servants, that with all boldness they may speak thy word, By stretching forth thine hand to heal; and that signs and wonders may be done by the name of thy holy child Jesus. This is an exact literal translation, and clearly proves that Jesus Christ, the Lord, by the Spirit, continued to heal the sick after Pentecost.

Since the very same Holy Spirit who raised Christ from the dead and who did all the miracles of the disciples dwells in us today, we can expect this same Jesus to continue His miraculous work by this same Spirit. Furthermore, many miracles have been witnessed in recent years, which show that God is still healing today.

Warfare Healing Principles

•• The most important thing in spiritual warfare is knowing what God's will is.

•• Praying for healing with the faith-destroying words, "If it be Thy will" is not warring. It is destroying the sick person.

•• Healing and salvation go hand in hand throughout Scripture.

•• God called sickness captivity.

•• Jesus called sickness bondage.

•• The Holy Spirit called sickness oppression.

•• When Christ died, He died for our sicknesses as well as for our sins.

•• Healing is in the atonement.

•• Jesus continues His healing ministry through His Body in the earth.

CHAPTER FIFTEEN
Building the Kingdom

It is not about building our own ministry, Church or kingdom. We are to build God's Kingdom and live with our minds set on things above.

Psalms 67:1, 2 To the chief Musician on Neginoth, A Psalm *or* Song. God be merciful unto us, and bless us; *and* cause his face to shine upon us; Selah. That thy way may be known upon earth, thy saving health among all nations.

I want to encourage you today with a word about Kingdom transformation. God desires to empower you, as His leader, to be an expression of His heart to all those around you. Today, God wants you to know that as He holds the whole world in the palm of His pierced hands, He also holds you, your family, your destiny, your dreams, your ministry and your vision along with every good gift and resource you could ever need.

John 17:12 While I was with them in the world, I kept them in thy name: those that thou gavest me I have kept, and none of them is lost, but the son of perdition; that the scripture might be fulfilled.

We need to have faith for the encounter to access the atmosphere of heaven, all we have to do is simply accept the Master's invitation to enter into the glory realm.

Matthew 17:1-13 And after six days Jesus taketh Peter, James, and John his brother, and bringeth them up into an high mountain apart, And was transfigured before them: and his face did shine as the sun, and his raiment was white as the light. And, behold, there appeared unto them Moses and Elias talking with him. Then answered Peter, and said unto Jesus, Lord, it is good for us to be here: if thou wilt, let us make here three tabernacles; one for thee, and one for Moses, and one for Elias. While he yet spake, behold, a bright cloud overshadowed them: and behold a voice out of the cloud, which said, This is my beloved Son, in whom I am well pleased; hear ye him. And when the disciples heard *it,* they fell on their face, and were sore afraid. And Jesus came and touched them, and said, Arise, and be not afraid. And when they had lifted up their eyes, they saw no man, save Jesus only. And as they came down from the mountain, Jesus charged them, saying, Tell the vision to no man, until the Son of man be risen again from the dead. And his disciples asked him, saying, Why then say the scribes that Elias must first come? And Jesus answered and said unto them, Elias truly shall first come, and restore all things. But I say unto you, That Elias is come already, and they knew him not, but have done unto him whatsoever they listed. Likewise shall also the Son of man suffer of them. Then the disciples understood that he spake unto them of John the Baptist.

Jesus took Peter, James and John up the mountain with Him and there the Lord was transfigured before them. His face shone like the sun and His clothes became shining bright and the glory of God was all around. In addition to this incredible sight, Moses and Elijah appeared before them and spoke with Jesus about His imminent departure from the earth.

The atmosphere of heaven causes a shift and brings with it an opening from heaven to earth. Mantles, miracles, salvations and healings are released when Messiah draws near. In the Prototype Church there will be open Heavens. More than ever before, God is calling His leaders to a fresh faith encounter in which we will be transformed into His likeness so that we can then lead others into similar God encounters.

At this time Peter suggested that he should put up three tents. We might say he wanted to 'build a monument to the moment', but God wasn't looking to build a monument; He was orchestrating a face to face encounter to facilitate Kingdom change beyond what they could ever imagine at this stage of their journey.

It was an awesome occurrence and we can understand why Peter wanted to keep hold of it forever!

God, however, had different ideas. He didn't want Peter to operate out of yesterday's anointing; God calls us to live in the 'now' of His eternal presence, invading every fiber of our being with His glory.

It is essential that leaders stay current with what is on God's agenda for the season they are appointed to. I have been in many meetings where the Minister talks about some miracle twenty years ago. If you stay connect to God you will have fresh fruit.

One potential leadership pitfall is to hold on to past ministry methods and "success" and consider it to be fresh manna, when in fact, God is pouring out fresh revelation, dreams, vision and calling every day. We can't keep everything the same or we get stale.

As Peter spoke a bright cloud enveloped them all and God's voice was clearly heard above Peter's.

Matthew 17:5 While he yet spake, behold, a bright cloud overshadowed them: and behold a voice out of the cloud, which said, This is my beloved Son, in whom I am well pleased; hear ye him.

Each one of us are legal royal sons and daughters, with an inheritance in Christ that can never spoil or perish.

God sought to ensure that the disciples recognized the strategic and significant nature of their encounter. With the coming death and resurrection of Christ, life as they knew it was going to change beyond recognition. This personal event in their lives was necessary to prepare them for what lay ahead. In time they would ultimately view this revelation of Christ's majesty in the wider context of reaching the multitudes.

There are times I believe when God is giving destiny downloads to anoint leaders and leaders in-training for divinely inspired activity. Like the disciples in this instance, we may not always immediately recognize such an encounter for what it is but in the fullness of time it will become evident.

By affirming Christ, God revealed Himself yet again as a loving Heavenly Father in touch with every aspect of His Son's life and the lives of all His children. By enveloping them in the glory cloud God included the 'trembling trio', simultaneously making it clear that it was not a time for idle chatter but a time to listen carefully to Christ, to comprehend his words and to act on faith based on their understanding of God's will.

God envelops us in His presence and in so doing we are made more effective as servant leaders. Every encounter with God has the potential within it to become a catalyst for impartation and transformation.

The disciples were terrified and fell face down when they heard God's voice but Jesus came and touched them in a reassuring manner. Not desiring that His disciples be ruled by fear He said, "*Don't be afraid*". You will have to overcome fear because as a leader you are at the forefront of God's army and Satan is going to confront you and attempt to intimidate you but God has a word for us – He did not give us a spirit of fear, but of power and of love and of sound mind! Experiencing fear is not to be considered a failure of faith: It is our response to fear that is crucial in our walk with Christ. We bring our fear to His feet and in prayer we learn to overcome and prevail in faith until breakthrough comes.

Jesus understands that fear can cause us to feel disengaged or even become apathetic or aggressive (passive or otherwise) to the process of change. The power of Christ's love breaks every fiber of fear in us. Jesus said to Peter, James and John, "*Get up*" because our Lord is passionate about active discipleship. He wants us on our feet, ready to respond to His voice and willing to move forward at any given time to His instruction. If we know who we are in God and who He is in us we will stand as fearless warriors.

Building a Prototype Church

Peter had come perilously close to building a memorial to the memory rather than realizing he was part of a Kingdom movement for change. We can all so easily fall prey to this religious mindset. Building a memorial to 'how things were' may prevent us from moving forward into the exciting new things God has for us.

We need to acknowledge that each touch of Christ is to maintain His divine momentum of transformation in us and through us. As leaders we cannot build for the future if we operate in the confused assumption that 'what was' is somehow better than 'what is' or 'what will be'.

Christ yearns to encounter us just as He did Peter, James and John on the Mount of Transfiguration. He calls us to keep moving; to finish what we've started; to press in for fresh vision and revelation; to collaborate with heaven and make divine connections for the advancement of His Kingdom here on earth. The disciples may have left the mountain without fully understanding what the future held. Nonetheless, God had imparted another revelation of His glory into their beings.

Every testimonial meeting with God is life changing even when we don't entirely 'get it'.

Our responses might initially look like Peter's – a little bit out of sync with God's direction but the Holy Spirit and the Word of God are our plumb-line in times of transition and enable us to respond to Him with humility and grace.

Take a moment to take stock of such encounters you may have had with the Lord, either recently or in the past, and allow the Holy Spirit to propel you into the next stage of your destiny as a leader in the body of Christ.

We must keep our focus in the right now and the future in the Glory of God. We are not to build a monument in this day. Monuments of religion are nothing that God looks for. Many will say in that day "I've prophesied in thy name done many wonderful works in thy name but God will say I NEVER KNEW YOU, DEPART FROM ME YOU WORK OF INIQUITY.

The lessons of Matthew 17 encouraged me not to become distracted by past glory moves of God nonetheless to give thanks for them and build upon their righteous foundations. I only look to past Glory as a reference. The past Glory is just to unlock the future Glory.

As I sought the Lord in prayer He graciously and immediately opened up the revelatory realms. Jesus truly does hold the whole world in His hands. God wants to encourage us to be a people with whom He can infuse His power and passion to partner Heaven in a Holy Spirit movement for change.

1Peter 1:23 Being born again, not of corruptible seed, but of incorruptible, by the word of God, which liveth and abideth for ever.

Today we have an opportunity to receive from our Master and become His agents for change.

You are called out, commissioned and empowered by the Holy Spirit to engage with heaven and effect change on the earth to the glory of God's name. You are called if you are reading this book to be part of this plan straight from Heaven.

2Corinthians 3:17, 18 Now the Lord is that Spirit: and where the Spirit of the Lord *is,* there *is* liberty. But we all, with open face beholding as in a glass the glory of the Lord, are changed into the same image from glory to glory, *even* as by the Spirit of the Lord.

As a leader I am extremely aware of the need to stay close to God and to be willing to embrace season of change that are Spirit led. As leaders we are often required to call others into times of transition; and God in turn asks that we would be willing to walk in the reality of pioneering and accepting change in our personal walk with Him, whether that change is pleasant or unpleasant, planned or unexpected.

Kairos Season becomes a Catalyst for Godly Change Jesus wrote another word in the sand: "KAIROS"

Luke 5:6, 7 And when they had this done, they inclosed a great multitude of fishes: and their net brake. And they beckoned unto *their* partners, which were in the other ship, that they should come and help them. And they came, and filled both the ships, so that they began to sink.

Romans 11:11, 12 I say then, Have they stumbled that they should fall? God forbid: but *rather* through their fall salvation *is come* unto the Gentiles, for to provoke them to jealousy. Now if the fall of them *be* the riches of the world, and the diminishing of them the riches of the Gentiles; how much more their fulness?

Isaiah 22:22 And the key of the house of David will I lay upon his shoulder; so he shall open, and none shall shut; and he shall shut, and none shall open.

Matthew 28:18-20 And Jesus came and spake unto them, saying, All power is given unto me in heaven and in earth. Go ye therefore, and teach all nations, baptizing them in the name of the Father, and of the Son, and of the Holy Ghost: Teaching them to observe all things whatsoever I have commanded you: and, lo, I am with you alway, *even* unto the end of the world. Amen.

Matthew 22:37-40 Jesus said unto him, Thou shalt love the Lord thy God with all thy heart, and with all thy soul, and with all thy mind. This is the first and great commandment. And the second *is* like unto it, Thou shalt love thy neighbour as thyself. On these two commandments hang all the law and the prophets.

2Corinthians 3:17, 18 Now the Lord is that Spirit: and where the Spirit of the Lord *is,* there *is* liberty. But we all, with open face beholding as in a glass the glory of the Lord, are changed into the same image from glory to glory, *even* as by the Spirit of the Lord.

I was deeply impacted as I reflected on the Lord's use of the combination of the elements of change and His *kairos* timing. The Greek word *kairos* refers to an appointed or set time or season, which is different to the Greek word *chronos*, which donates a more general period of time. A quick Bible word search will reveal that when the *kairos* time of God comes upon His servants, truly there is acceleration!

The angel Gabriel when speaking to Zechariah of the birth of his future son indicated that his words would be fulfilled in their season (*kairos*) *Luke 1:20*; Promises from God find their fulfilment in His *kairos* timing.

The prophet Amos spoke of the *kairos* time of God in relation to the outpouring of new wine, i.e. when the plough man (harvester) shall overtake the reaper.

Amos 9:13 Behold, the days come, saith the LORD, that the plowman shall overtake the reaper, and the treader of grapes him that soweth seed; and the mountains shall drop sweet wine, and all the hills shall melt.

Harvest seasons bring forth glory multiplication from heaven to earth in the *kairos* timing of God. The *kairos* timing of God thrusts us beyond believing for breakthrough into experientially receiving our breakthrough. *Kairos* timing, therefore, becomes a catalyst for Godly change that ushers in His glory.

Matthew 17:2 And was transfigured before them: and his face did shine as the sun, and his raiment was white as the light.

The Greek word used here is *metamorphoo*, which means to transform, change or transfigure.

God wants us to understand that in our season of divinely appointed change, He is transforming us in, to and through His glory. What a revelation of grace and glory to the church – we are in a season of holy metamorphosis and what a wonderful word of encouragement to leaders today!

Chapter Sixteen
Fasting Transforms Lives

Many people fast but we must keep the proper principles in line or we are just not eating for any reason. When you obey God through prayer and fasting, He has promised blessings of provision, success, good health, restoration, deliverance, victory over enemies and more.

I've seen God's faithfulness in action. This principle really works!

I opened the windows of Heaven through prayer and fasting. I want you to experience the rewards of this important biblical principle. I would fast only by the direction of the Holy Spirit.

Whether you are considering your very first fast or wanting to go to a deeper spiritual level with your fast, this Chapter will provide the encouragement and practical information from God's Word you need to make your effort a success.

Not only does fasting bring success in your daily life, but I believe it also opens your heart to God's voice. Your life will never be the same. Fasting works!

Fasting, prayer and reading God's Word go hand in hand. When you fast, also pray for God's purpose and plan for your life to be revealed. Fast and pray about every major decision in your life. Simply put, fasting is a way to conquer the physical and open the door to the supernatural in your life.

Many fast by skipping meals but there is no extra time of prayer. I'm telling you if you are fasting you must press into God.

When you deny your body, you feed your spirit and grow closer to the Lord.

In Matthew 6, Jesus gave us specific direction on how to live as a child of God. That pattern addressed three specific duties of a Christian: Giving, Praying and Fasting. Jesus said, "When you give," "when you pray," "when you fast." He made it clear that fasting, like giving and praying, was a normal part of Christian life.

I believe that when all three disciplines—giving, praying and fasting—are at work in your life, you release the complete power of God.

Mark 4:8 And other fell on good ground, and did yield fruit that sprang up and increased; and brought forth, some thirty, and some sixty, and some an hundred.

When you pray, you release the thirty-fold return. Praying and giving releases sixty-fold blessing. But when you pray, give and fast, you will see a hundred-fold return!

Before beginning a fast, write down a plan and make a verbal commitment to the Lord. When you approach it with determination, you'll be less likely to waiver in weak moments.

You may be surprised to find that fasting is not as intimidating as you may think. But if you do find it to be a battle, don't lose heart, God knows your weaknesses.

His fasting principles allow you the flexibility to take care of your job and duties while still making a sacrifice to honor Him.

If the traditional full fast has always made you shy away from this important principle, you may be surprised to know that there are actually many different types of fasts. Find the fast or combination of fasts that fits your needs.

For example, if you choose to go on a 21-day fast, you may want to begin with a full fast for 1-3 days and then continue with a

Daniel Fast or some other type of partial fast for the remainder of the 21 days.

No matter which fast you decide on, you must always remember to consult your doctor and drink lots of water.

FULL FAST. Drink only liquids – especially water. On this type of fast you may also take in clear broth and 100 percent fruit or vegetable juices in order to maintain your strength.

You establish the number of days for your fast in your prayer time. Be sure to consult your doctor.

PARTIAL FAST. There are many options for partial fasts. Here are just a few for you to select from.

Daniel Fast: The most frequently used example of a partial fast, found in Daniel, chapter 10, the Daniel Fast is a fast from meats, sweets, breads and any drink, except water, for a specific time period

Daniel 10:2, 3 In those days I Daniel was mourning three full weeks. I ate no pleasant bread, neither came flesh nor wine in my mouth, neither did I anoint myself at all, till three whole weeks were fulfilled.

The easiest way to think of this fast is you should eat vegetables, fruits and drink only water. Be sure to consult your doctor, especially if you have any medical condition.

Here are examples of other types of partial fasts. But remember, the type of fast you select is what you and the Lord agree upon.

* give up one item of food or drink such as caffeine, coffee, soft drinks or sweets or give up one meal.

* fast for a specific number of days . . .one day, three days, so on.

* choose to fast from 6 a.m. to 3 p.m. or from sun-up to sundown. When doing this type of fast, consider your work and sleep schedule.

The hours that you sleep should not be considered part of your fasting period, so the timeframe for this type of fast may vary.

The Lord speaks of Private fasts and Corporate fasts in Scripture.

CORPORATE FAST. A Corporate fast is a joint fast of believers for a specific purpose that can yield powerful results.

Although this fast involves others, it is also very much a "private and personal experience." Esther called all of her people to fast for protection against danger.

Ester 4:16 Go, gather together all the Jews that are present in Shushan, and fast ye for me, and neither eat nor drink three days, night or day: I also and my maidens will fast likewise; and so will I go in unto the king, which *is* not according to the law: and if I perish, I perish.

Samuel declared a fast for national revival.

1Samuel 1:7 And *as* he did so year by year, when she went up to the house of the LORD, so she provoked her; therefore she wept, and did not eat.

If you want to make fasting a way of life, work out a plan for the entire year to include days or meals to fast that works into your lifestyle.

You may decide to fast one day a month or one meal a week. You may even decide to do a partial fast for one week every other month.

Options are endless. There are also other unexpected times that you may feel a need to fast—during family struggles, financial problems, etc. Specific times when you need to capture the attention and mercy of God in your life.

The best way to show your children the power of fasting is to lead by example.

If they want to participate in fasting or if you want to have a family fast, consider giving up desserts, electronics or soft drinks.

In addition to giving up an item of food, you could also give up television as a family and spend that time reading and discussing the Bible.

Seeking God through prayer and fasting is never a waste of time. Try finishing up with a partial fast if you cannot make it to the end. You should repent since you fell short of your commitment.

Moderate exercise is good. But it is best to always consult a doctor about fasting and exercise.

If you are on a complete fast, you may not have the energy for a high level of exercise.

If you have a job that requires you to expend a lot of physical energy, you may want to consider a partial fast that allows you to receive enough nutrition to perform your job.

1Corinthians 7:2-5 Nevertheless, *to avoid* fornication, let every man have his own wife, and let every woman have her own husband. Let the husband render unto the wife due benevolence: and likewise also the wife unto the husband. The wife hath not power of her own body, but the husband: and likewise also the husband hath not power of his own body, but the wife. Defraud ye not one the other, except *it be* with consent for a time, that ye may give yourselves to fasting and prayer; and come together again, that Satan tempt you not for your incontinency.

EXCEPT WITH CONSENT, for a time that you may give yourselves to fasting and prayer. So the answer is yes.

Scripture allows this for the purpose of fasting and prayer, BUT only with mutual consent. Wherever you are in life or whatever your needs today, fasting can benefit you.

If you are struggling with your health or finances, fasting is a powerful spiritual tool. Maybe you need guidance from God or protection for your family. Fasting is a private discipline with public rewards.

It is the spiritual key in certain seasons and situations of your life. Whatever your season in life, release the power of fasting into your needs.

Fasting gives you the opportunity to pray and intercede specifically for your family. It's important to fast and pray for your children's and grandchildren's future.

God is looking for men and women with fervent prayer lives who will do spiritual battle on behalf of their families!

Fasting will open your eyes to the needs of your family. The Lord will point out the needs of your family members from deep within your heart and soul, such as encouragement for your spouse or special prayer and attention for a child. You can fast and pray specifically for a protective covering of safety around your family.

Ester 4:16 Go, gather together all the Jews that are present in Shushan, and fast ye for me, and neither eat nor drink three days, night or day: I also and my maidens will fast likewise; and so will I go in unto the king, which *is* not according to the law: and if I perish, I perish.

If you face a financial struggle that seems insurmountable, you are not alone. Ezra faced a big problem with the silver and gold he was responsible for.

Ezra 7:14-17 Forasmuch as thou art sent of the king, and of his seven counsellors, to enquire concerning Judah and Jerusalem, according to the law of thy God which *is* in thine hand; And to carry the silver and gold, which the king and his counsellors have freely offered unto the God of Israel, whose habitation *is* in Jerusalem, And all the silver and gold that thou canst find in all the province of Babylon, with the freewill offering of the people, and of the priests, offering willingly for the house of their God which *is* in Jerusalem:

That thou mayest buy speedily with this money bullocks, rams, lambs, with their meat offerings and their drink offerings, and offer them upon the altar of the house of your God which *is* in Jerusalem.

Maybe you feel like thieves have stolen what belongs to you financially. When Ezra faced an uncertain financial journey, he declared a fast and God answered his prayer!

Ezra 8:21 Then I proclaimed a fast there, at the river of Ahava, that we might afflict ourselves before our God, to seek of him a right way for us, and for our little ones, and for all our substance.

If you will fast, pray and obey God's commandments, He said you will be blessed.

Deuteronomy 28:2 And all these blessings shall come on thee, and overtake thee, if thou shalt hearken unto the voice of the LORD thy God.

The widow also faced an uncertain future. Although the woman had very little, she gave up her own food to help Elijah, the man of God.

1Kings 17:10-16 So he arose and went to Zarephath. And when he came to the gate of the city, behold, the widow woman *was* there gathering of sticks: and he called to her, and said, Fetch me, I pray thee, a little water in a vessel, that I may drink. And as she was going to fetch *it,* he called to her, and said, Bring me, I pray thee, a morsel of bread in thine hand. And she said, *As* the LORD thy God liveth, I have not a cake, but an handful of meal in a barrel, and a little oil in a cruse: and, behold, I *am* gathering two sticks, that I may go in and dress it for me and my son, that we may eat it, and die. And Elijah said unto her, Fear not; go *and* do as thou hast said: but make me thereof a little cake first, and bring *it* unto me, and after make for thee and for thy son. For thus saith the LORD God of Israel, The barrel of meal shall not waste, neither shall the cruse of oil fail, until the day *that* the LORD sendeth rain upon the earth. And she went and did according to the saying of Elijah: and she, and he, and her house, did eat *many* days. *And* the barrel of meal wasted not, neither did the cruse of oil fail, according to the word of the LORD, which he spake by Elijah.

Remember the widow? God multiplied the meal in her barrel to last for three and a half years!

In Mark, chapter 9, Christ's disciples were frustrated because they could not cast out an evil spirit.

Mark 9:29 And he said unto them, This kind can come forth by nothing, but by prayer and fasting.

If you are afflicted with addictions or sin, you can go on a fast that frees you from besetting sins.

Hebrews 12:1 Wherefore seeing we also are compassed about with so great a cloud of witnesses, let us lay aside every weight, and the sin which doth so easily beset *us,* and let us run with patience the race that is set before us,

Besetting sins are those that ensnare us and hinder us from achieving God's purpose for our lives. Through fasting we can break free from the addictions and habits that are not pleasing to God.

Isaiah 58:6 *Is* not this the fast that I have chosen? to loose the bands of wickedness, to undo the heavy burdens, and to let the oppressed go free, and that ye break every yoke?

Christ said the key to deliverance from sin is fasting and prayer. Maybe you struggle with the emotional bondage of depression or anxiety. Elijah also battled negative emotional feelings. When Jezebel sent word that she wanted to kill Elijah, he became distraught. He was depressed and even suicidal.

1Kings 19:4 But he himself went a day's journey into the wilderness, and came and sat down under a juniper tree: and he requested for himself that he might die; and said, It is enough; now, O LORD, take away my life; for I *am* not better than my fathers.

An angel came to Elijah and instructed him to journey back into the presence of God. The Bible says that Elijah fasted for 40 days and 40 nights as he returned to Horeb, the mountain of God. God delivered Elijah from feelings of suicide and fear.

He gave Him hope, courage and direction.

Are you faced with a major life decision and don't know what to do? Maybe you have a job opportunity a broken relationship or an unfulfilled dream. Fasting can help you clear away the clutter of life and discern God's voice. Saul was going the wrong direction in life. He was hunting down followers of Christ and persecuting them when the light of God's truth knocked him off his path.

Acts 9:3 And as he journeyed, he came near Damascus: and suddenly there shined round about him a light from heaven: And he fell to the earth, and heard a voice saying unto him, Saul, Saul, why persecutest thou me? And he said, Who art thou, Lord? And the Lord said, I am Jesus whom thou persecutest: *it is* hard for thee to kick against the pricks. And he trembling and astonished said, Lord, what wilt thou have me to do? And the Lord *said* unto him, Arise, and go into the city, and it shall be told thee what thou must do.

Acts 9:9 And he was three days without sight, and neither did eat nor drink.

He didn't know what to do, but he fasted for God's divine direction. Then God sent the disciple Ananias to him with guidance.

Acts 9:17 And Ananias went his way, and entered into the house; and putting his hands on him said, Brother Saul, the Lord, *even* Jesus, that appeared unto thee in the way as thou camest, hath sent me, that thou mightest receive thy sight, and be filled with the Holy Ghost.

Through this process Saul became Paul, one of God's chosen apostles. Through his fast, Paul received the direction he needed and so can you. When you don't know what to do or when you face a daunting decision, that's when you need to fast and pray fervently for God's direction.

The Bible gives us a perfect example of how denying ourselves physically can bring good health. It is the story of Daniel and his peers.

Daniel 1:12 Prove thy servants, I beseech thee, ten days; and let them give us pulse to eat, and water to drink.

Daniel 10:2, 3 In those days I Daniel was mourning three full weeks. I ate no pleasant bread, neither came flesh nor wine in my mouth, neither did I anoint myself at all, till three whole weeks were fulfilled.

This fast is a partial and a prolonged fast that yields health and healing.

Daniel 1:15 And at the end of ten days their countenances appeared fairer and fatter in flesh than all the children which did eat the portion of the king's meat.

Daniel and his men were healthier! If you have a physical problem, fast for healing.

When Samuel took over as priest and judge over the nation, he declared a fast for national revival. Samuel told the people to fast and seek God to return His presence to the nation.

1Samuel 7:3 And Samuel spake unto all the house of Israel, saying, If ye do return unto the LORD with all your hearts, *then* put away the strange gods and Ashtaroth from among you, and prepare your hearts unto the LORD, and serve him only: and he will deliver you out of the hand of the Philistines.

Our society today critically needs believers who will fast and pray for revival.

2Chronicles 7:14 If my people, which are called by my name, shall humble themselves, and pray, and seek my face, and turn from their wicked ways; then will I hear from heaven, and will forgive their sin, and will heal their land.

We can return God's presence and glory to our personal lives and our nations; will you do your part? Fast, pray and seek Him now.

John the Baptist and his disciples fasted often, according to Matthew 9.

Matthew 3:1-4 In those days came John the Baptist, preaching in the wilderness of Judaea, And saying, Repent ye: for the kingdom of heaven is at hand. For this is he that was spoken of by the prophet Esaias, saying, The voice of one crying in the wilderness, Prepare ye the way of the Lord, make his paths straight. And the same John had his raiment of camel's hair, and a leathern girdle about his loins; and his meat was locusts and wild honey.

Because of John the Baptist's constant fasting, I believe he had a greater testimony and influence on the lives of people in his generation than any other man.

Matthew 11:1 And it came to pass, when Jesus had made an end of commanding his twelve disciples, he departed thence to teach and to preach in their cities.

John 1:6, 7 There was a man sent from God, whose name *was* John. The same came for a witness, to bear witness of the Light, that all *men* through him might believe.

If you and I want to win the lost in our communities, in our nation and around the world, we must do spiritual warfare through fasting and prayer. When you deny yourself and focus on God's will through prayer, He will begin to open doors of evangelism in your life.

Understand Fasting can be anything as long as you press into God during that fast. You should seek the Lord to see if a fast is in order before you begin a long fast. Here are some things other than food that I have fasted that has changed my life.

Coffee

Television

Friends

Computer

Soda

The Church is in a Season of Profound of Change

Believe it or not these things were harder than food. We all need set free of too much of all these things.

Chapter Seventeen
Misusing the Prophetic Gift

I have seen much abuse of the Gift called prophecy. This happens a lot in the Body of Christ. Unfortunately, many "sell" their giftings to the highest bidder.

I love the prophetic gift. I confess that miracles, signs, and wonders make me giddy, but they cannot be bought and sold like some cheap dollar store toys. We are accountable for how we treat them. If anyone abuses their gift sooner or later you will lose it. I constantly keep my gift in check with the Holy Spirit. If you surround yourself with prophetic people it will be a safe guard. They can judge us if we begin to stray from the pure gift of prophecy.

Maybe we let it just slide here and there. Maybe someone gives a good, cushy prophetic word to someone important and it's really "thus says the prophet" verses "thus says the Lord."

We as the prophetic people of God must be separate. We must continually strive to give the pure word of the Lord instead of giving what people want to hear.

I am saddened time and time again when people come to me wanting a "word" about a particular instance. While I flow in a prophetic gifting from God, I am not a psychic. I do not perform on demand. I wait for His command. I can pray with someone about a situation, but I cannot force anything to happen. I do not, as a prophetic voice, get to pick and choose what God wants to tell people. I do, however, believe that God always has something to say to His people, much like a father has for his child.

The Church is in a Season of Profound of Change

I know prophetic people that won't prophecy to certain people because of the bad feelings they have for them. I prophesy to all those God tells me. They may have talked bad about me, left my Church wrongly etc. and I still give them the Word God has for them.

However, we must be very careful not to conjure up words for a person just because we want to. The prophetic voice has to mature and learn when to say something, how to say it, and when not to. I've gotten this right before, and I've messed up, too. There is a responsibility involved in being the mouthpiece of God. We have to learn to give the word the way God wants it given. We have to learn when to say something and when to be silent and pray.

I am just the vessel. I teach people that often in the prophetic we are just the mail carrier. We give the mail. We don't have to understand the word or even attempt to, but let the person who it's for understand it. We stay out of it. All too often, I've seen prophetic people think that they need to either understand the word or hear the person's life story after something like this. The prophetic voice doesn't need to know everything. The good news is that God knows everything, and when it's God, it works. Stop trying to make a prophetic word fit into the vessel you think it should, but allow God to reveal Himself through it. If we are not careful, we'll become like a frustrated person doing a puzzle. It's an easy trap to fall into, but all too often we can try to bang in the prophetic word to make it fit into our own places. Really all we're doing is setting up problems for later.

We must realize that in the new Prototype Church there is going to be a new found structure of the prophetic.

The Bible says we all can prophesy and should prophesy but many shouldn't release a Word unless they know it is God.

Many people have this misguided view that the measure of a prophetic individual's accuracy is the measure in which that person is acceptable to God. That is a false teaching and mindset that affects the Church. The Bible talks a lot about false prophets. Balaam is just the tip of that iceberg.

Jeremiah 14:14 Then the LORD said unto me, The prophets prophesy lies in my name: I sent them not, neither have I commanded them, neither spake unto them: they prophesy unto you a false vision and divination, and a thing of nought, and the deceit of their heart.

Matthew 7:15 Beware of false prophets, which come to you in sheep's clothing, but inwardly they are ravening wolves.

Matthew 24:24 For there shall arise false Christs, and false prophets, and shall shew great signs and wonders; insomuch that, if *it were* possible, they shall deceive the very elect.

Ezekiel 22:28 And her prophets have daubed them with untempered *morter,* seeing vanity, and divining lies unto them, saying, Thus saith the Lord GOD, when the LORD hath not spoken.

Sadly, many false prophets go around in the Body of Christ today, parading themselves as true prophets. They wear the right clothes and they say the right things at all the right times, but it is a lie. Sometimes it can be very hard to discern the difference between a prophet of God and a false prophet. Accuracy is not the measure of a true prophet. You will know the true prophets by their fruit. Beware of false prophets, which come to you in sheep's clothing, but inwardly they are ravening wolves. Ye shall know them by their fruits. Do men gather grapes of thorns, or figs of thistles? Even so every good tree bringeth forth good fruit; but a corrupt tree bringeth forth evil fruit.

Matthew 17:15-20 Lord, have mercy on my son: for he is lunatick, and sore vexed: for ofttimes he falleth into the fire, and oft into the water. And I brought him to thy disciples, and they could not cure him. Then Jesus answered and said, O faithless and perverse generation, how long shall I be with you? how long shall I suffer you? bring him hither to me. And Jesus rebuked the devil; and he departed out of him: and the child was cured from that very hour. Then came the disciples to Jesus apart, and said, Why could not we cast him out? And Jesus said unto them, Because of your unbelief: for verily I say unto you, If ye have faith as a grain of mustard seed, ye shall say unto this mountain, Remove hence to yonder place; and it shall remove; and nothing shall be impossible unto you.

If you can't tell if a prophetic voice is false or not, look at the fruit born from the word or the situation. Check the Fruit!

Sadly, true prophets have gotten a bad rap today. So many people have misused the Holy Spirit and have been like Balaam; too many have closed their hearts to the prophetic. I assure you, God still uses Godly men and women with character to speak His words to His Church and His people. Just because there have been a few bad apples in the bunch doesn't mean we should burn the entire bushel of apples. Just remove the bad apples.

I'm not diving into the divination side of Balaam's story, which does go on in a lot in churches. I think that side is pretty cut and dry—stop doing it. The issue with Balaam is not just that he used divination, which is wrong. The spirit of Balaam showed through when Balaam saw those Israelites struggling and he preferred to curse them than to help them. He wasn't trying to meet them and greet them. Balaam could have cared less about the Israelites. He was all about himself. He wanted his fee and didn't really care about the people. He would rather throw stumbling blocks in front of them than help them. That heart motive is the focus of this book. We must guard our gifts and keep them pure.

Chapter Eighteen
Obedience – Not Sacrifice

In becoming a Prototype Church we have to be obedient in everything we do to God. My wife can tell you I'm ridiculously obedient in everything. In my personal life I was crying out with a deep desire to know God for who He was as opposed to what He could do for me. God began to introduce me to holiness and the crucified life, concepts that were nearly strange to me.

I went to press in for hours and after several minutes of dry silence, God spoke, "Bill, I don't want your five hours of sacrifice. I want obedience!" These words riveted me. I lay speechless before a holy God. How could I have been so deceived to count the minutes. How could I have treated His desire and will so lightly! I had chosen a carnal thing over obeying God.

Matthew 16:24 Then said Jesus unto his disciples, If any *man* will come after me, let him deny himself, and take up his cross, and follow me.

Some take up the cross and concentrate on its image of suffering, which represents a life of sacrifice. However, in this verse the cross is not the end result. It enables us to obey. You can live a life of denial and sacrifice yet not "follow Him." In fact, you could choose denial and sacrifice and still be in rebellion against God!

The focus of what Jesus is saying is obedience! The only way we can obey is to take up the cross. For without death to our own agendas and desires we will eventually have a face-off between the will of God and the desire of man. If we do not lay down our lives we will find a way of fulfilling our own wills and even use scriptures to back it!

Sacrifice was scriptural, so Saul was scriptural in his desire to sacrifice animals as offerings. But he was disobedient to God's directive. Does service to God include disobedience? If so, Satan would receive glory from our "scriptural" religious practices or sacrifices. He is the originator of rebellion.

1Samuel 15:22 And Samuel said, Hath the LORD *as great* delight in burnt offerings and sacrifices, as in obeying the voice of the LORD? Behold, to obey *is* better than sacrifice, *and* to hearken than the fat of rams.

Have you ever gone on a job interview? You put on your best clothing, labor over your hair, and carry a roll of breath mints. Why? Because of the status of the person you're about to meet. Before Isaiah discusses obedience and sacrifice, he gives us a glimpse of the One we're being asked to obey.

1Kings 8:27 But will God indeed dwell on the earth? behold, the heaven and heaven of heavens cannot contain thee; how much less this house that I have builded?

Isaiah 40:12 Who hath measured the waters in the hollow of his hand, and meted out heaven with the span, and comprehended the dust of the earth in a measure, and weighed the mountains in scales, and the hills in a balance?

Ecclesiastes 3:14 I know that, whatsoever God doeth, it shall be for ever: nothing can be put to it, nor any thing taken from it: and God doeth *it,* that *men* should fear before him.

There's a big difference between the works that we do and the works that God does. When God does it, nothing can be added, and nothing can be subtracted.

Psalms 127:1 A Song of degrees for Solomon. Except the LORD build the house, they labour in vain that build it: except the LORD keep the city, the watchman waketh *but* in vain.

Nothing changes or takes away from God's plans. Even if we labor in vain or set ourselves against His purposes, His intentions will be fulfilled.

Joseph's ten older brothers assumed that when they sold Joseph into slavery, they aborted God's plan to make Joseph a ruler. However, their evil scheme actually brought forth the fulfillment of God's plan.

Solomon said:

Ecclesiastes 3:15 That which hath been is now; and that which is to be hath already been; and God requireth that which is past.

The course is set already. That which is and that which is to come has already been in the mind of God. This shows His sovereignty. But God does require an account of what is past. This is to say, we will account for our obedience or disobedience to His ordained will.

This illustrates the free will of man. Some will say, "If this is the case, then man can subtract from what God does by just not doing what He planned." No, because God knows the end from the beginning. He knows what each person will do before they do it. He does not author it, for He is not the author of evil. But He does use it in His majestic wisdom. Hallelujah! Are you glimpsing His glory?

There are two ways a person can disobey. First, when you do what God has not told you to do and, second, when you do not do what you've been told to do. This is why Solomon said, "And God requires an account of what is past."

We are all son's we obey God's ways. Jesus did no more or less than what He saw His Father do. He did not add to or take away from it, which was in complete contrast to the religious leaders of His day.

The Church is in a Season of Profound of Change

Examine closely these two quotes of Jesus, making note of the word nothing:

John 15:19 If ye were of the world, the world would love his own: but because ye are not of the world, but I have chosen you out of the world, therefore the world hateth you.

John 5:30 I can of mine own self do nothing: as I hear, I judge: and my judgment is just; because I seek not mine own will, but the will of the Father which hath sent me.

Jesus did not minister for the first thirty years of His life. Can you imagine it? He knew He was the Messiah when He was twelve. We know this because His parents found Him in the temple listening and asking questions. When they asked Him why, He responded, "Did you not know that I must be about My Father's business?" He then went home with them and was subject to them until the age of thirty. We further confirm this by the fact that His first miracle was at the age of thirty at the wedding of Cana.

Luke 2:41-52 Now his parents went to Jerusalem every year at the feast of the passover. And when he was twelve years old, they went up to Jerusalem after the custom of the feast. And when they had fulfilled the days, as they returned, the child Jesus tarried behind in Jerusalem; and Joseph and his mother knew not *of it*. But they, supposing him to have been in the company, went a day's journey; and they sought him among *their* kinsfolk and acquaintance. And when they found him not, they turned back again to Jerusalem, seeking him. And it came to pass, that after three days they found him in the temple, sitting in the midst of the doctors, both hearing them, and asking them questions. And all that heard him were astonished at his understanding and answers. And when they saw him, they were amazed: and his mother said unto him, Son, why hast thou thus dealt with us? behold, thy father and I have sought thee sorrowing. And he said unto them, How is it that ye sought me? wist ye not that I must be about my Father's business? And they understood not the saying which he spake unto them. And he went down with them, and came to Nazareth, and was subject unto them: but his mother kept all these sayings in her heart. And Jesus increased in wisdom and stature, and in favour with God and man.

John 2:11 This beginning of miracles did Jesus in Cana of Galilee, and manifested forth his glory; and his disciples believed on him.

Can you see Him as a twenty-five-year-old man as He passed the blind, deaf, crippled, and leprous lining the streets of Nazareth? He could have laid hands on them and healed them. But He did not. He waited. He made furniture, faithfully attended synagogue, and roamed the hills of Galilee in prayer until He was thirty. Not launching Himself or His ministry, He waited for the Father's ordination.

Matthew 3:17 And lo a voice from heaven, saying, This is my beloved Son, in whom I am well pleased.

Well pleased! He hadn't done anything but making furniture and walking the hills of Galilee. Yet the reason for God's pleasure was Jesus' perfect obedience in all things, even if these did not include what we would call ministry.

Now look forward at His ministry. There are many incidents that reflect His perfect obedience. Let's look at a few:

John 11:1-6 Now a certain *man* was sick, *named* Lazarus, of Bethany, the town of Mary and her sister Martha. (It was *that* Mary which anointed the Lord with ointment, and wiped his feet with her hair, whose brother Lazarus was sick.) Therefore his sisters sent unto him, saying, Lord, behold, he whom thou lovest is sick. When Jesus heard *that,* he said, This sickness is not unto death, but for the glory of God, that the Son of God might be glorified thereby. Now Jesus loved Martha, and her sister, and Lazarus. When he had heard therefore that he was sick, he abode two days still in the same place where he was.

The messengers probably argued, "Maybe we did not make it clear, Jesus. He is so sick that he will die! You must hurry!" Yet Jesus wasn't moved. The sun set on the first day, and all those around Him looked at each other with questions in their eyes, "Doesn't Jesus care? Why hasn't He left for Bethany? It's been hours since we told Him the news. What kind of friend is He?" Jesus sensed their questions and disappointment, yet He still didn't move.

Notice the marked difference between Jesus' lack of action and Saul's make-it-happen, make-them-happy mind-set. Saul knew God's command but was unable to handle the pressure of the people. He gave in and gave them what they wanted.

1Samuel 15:24 And Saul said unto Samuel, I have sinned: for I have transgressed the commandment of the LORD, and thy words: because I feared the people, and obeyed their voice.

He appeased men yet disobeyed God. How often do we disobey our Father to appease our brothers?

Jesus did only what His Father said! After two days passed, Jesus said, "Let's go to Lazarus."

John 5:19 Then answered Jesus and said unto them, Verily, verily, I say unto you, The Son can do nothing of himself, but what he seeth the Father do: for what things soever he doeth, these also doeth the Son likewise.

John 12:26 If any man serve me, let him follow me; and where I am, there shall also my servant be: if any man serve me, him will *my* Father honour.

We have mistakenly thought that if we laid hands on the sick, independent of the Spirit's leading; God was obligated to heal and confirm our lead by following with His signs. If this were true, we should go empty the hospitals. We get discouraged when God does not follow our lead with His healing and miracles. God will heal and perform miracles, but it is as He leads and we follow. There are many references in the Gospels of, "He healed them all." But they were not general occurrences. Take, for instance, all the sick, blind, lame, and paralyzed people Jesus left at the pool of Bethesda after He healed the man with the infirmity of thirty-eight years. Why did He walk in and heal the one and not touch the rest?

How about the man, lame from his mother's womb, who was laid daily at the gate of the temple? Jesus passed him each time He entered the temple. Why didn't Jesus heal him? Because His Father hadn't instructed Him to do so. Yet it was God's will for this man to be healed. Later Peter and John raised him up under the direction of the Holy Spirit.

Neither did Jesus minister by formulas. He spit on one, laid hands on some, and simply spoke to others. He formed balls of mud and placed them in eye sockets and sent others to the priests.

Why the variety? Because He wasn't following a formula—He was doing what He saw His Father do! This is how God wants His children to serve Him. He desires us to come to the place where we will only do what we see Him do. That includes doing nothing when God is silent. He longs for us to leave behind the sacrifices based on what we think, want, or are pressured to do and return to simple obedience to Him.

Remember, Isaiah pointed out that all our sacrifice can't give God anything He doesn't already have.

Isaiah 66:1, 2 Thus saith the LORD, The heaven *is* my throne, and the earth *is* my footstool: where *is* the house that ye build unto me? and where *is* the place of my rest? For all those *things* hath mine hand made, and all those *things* have been, saith the LORD: but to this *man* will I look, *even* to *him that is* poor and of a contrite spirit, and trembleth at my word.

When we are overwhelmed by our inadequacies, our awesome Father promises to pay attention and uphold the humble man who trembles at His word. The humblest, meekest man is the one who gets God's attention.

Here is a revealing list containing some of the characteristics of one who trembles at God's word:

1. Obedience is immediate.

2. God's will is honored above all else.

3. There is no arguing, complaining, or pouting.

4. They search for the heartbeat of God.

5. When God's will is unclear, they wait until it is.

6. They suffer the rejection of friends rather than displease God.

7. They do not add or take away from what God says.

8. There is awe for God's ways and wisdom, for there is none greater.

Isaiah tells us in graphic terms about God's attitude toward sacrifices that are not out of obedience.

Isaiah 66:3 He that killeth an ox *is as if* he slew a man; he that sacrificeth a lamb, *as if* he cut off a dog's neck; he that offereth an oblation, *as if he offered* swine's blood; he that burneth incense, *as if* he blessed an idol. Yea, they have chosen their own ways, and their soul delighteth in their abominations.

Didn't God ordain the lamb sacrifices? Wasn't He the One who ordained the grain offering? Wasn't it God who instructed Moses to burn incense in the holy place of the tabernacle? So why now does He compare the sacrifice of the lamb and bull to the killing of a man or the breaking of a dog's neck? Why does He say their offerings are like an unclean pig's blood? Why does He liken the incense offered (a shadow of their worship and prayer) to the blessing of an idol? Just as they have chosen their own ways, And their soul delights in their abominations, So will I choose their delusions, And bring their fears on them; Because, when I called, no one answered, When I spoke they did not hear; But they did evil before My eyes, And chose that in which I do not delight.

Isaiah 66:3, 4 He that killeth an ox *is as if* he slew a man; he that sacrificeth a lamb, *as if* he cut off a dog's neck; he that offereth an oblation, *as if he offered* swine's blood; he that burneth incense, *as if* he blessed an idol. Yea, they have chosen their own ways, and their soul delighteth in their abominations. I also will choose their delusions, and will bring their fears upon them; because when I called, none did answer; when I spake, they did not hear: but they did evil before mine eyes, and chose *that* in which I delighted not.

He made it clear that His delight is not in sacrifice!

What about today? Are we so busy serving God with intercessory prayer, generous offerings, orderly services, outreaches, ministry administration, fasting, Bible studies, Christian conferences and conventions that we are missing what He is saying? Caught up in it all, have we lost the simplicity of hearing His voice and trembling at His word? Today it is very easy to build a ministry machine yet lose the focus of its purpose. It is easy to succumb to the pressure of work-loads, financial obligations, maintaining our status, the demands of controlling people, and all else that tries to dictate our course, but what about obedience to the Spirit of God?

Can we follow as He leads, or are we bound by charismatic, full gospel service order? Perhaps our services are not ordered by a written bulletin such as is the case in many denominations, but the truth is many nondenominational churches have set service orders, too—they just are not written out. So we scorn those who are honest enough to write out their order of service, judging them as "bound and not free like us."

Our order is clear. It's praise, then worship (by the way, praise is the fast songs and worship is the slow ones, in case you're not sure what the difference is), followed by announcements, offering, the message, altar call, and possibly laying hands on some people in the hope they will fall over. We boast in this freedom of worship. But in actuality we've been delivered from hymnals only to be bound to transparencies. Yet all the while we believe ourselves to be Spirit-led.

The Church is in a Season of Profound of Change

This attitude places us in a vulnerable position. We become highly susceptible to the type of disobedience found in King Saul, believing that having all components for ministry is more crucial than obedience to God. In this setting God will not compete for our attention. He stands back and watches as we carry on. This is not limited to ministry alone. It occurs on a personal level as well.

We must remember that a thousand acts of obedience do not justify one act of disobedience! That I could have been so ignorant and arrogant now makes me want to scream. Jesus gave His very life for me, and I smugly judged His leading as optional because of my menial works! May God keep us from the subtle deception that leads to disobedience! I thank God I found my way and pray that the Holy Spirit will keep me on the path of God through obedience.

Chapter Nineteen
Ministry Women Come Forth

Should a Woman Serve as Pastor or a minister? The proposed revision to the many Faiths and Message states, "the office of pastor is limited to men."

I tell you if we really are going to be a Prototype Church we can only do this with women and children in place of ministry.

Current Church leader was quoted "Our positions and our perspectives are not going to be dictated by the culture. They're going to be dictated by Scripture. If we stand alone, we'll stand alone." There you have it. Those who believe the Bible reject women pastors, and those who give in to culture accept women pastors.

Such thinking is arrogant nonsense. They should have said, "I believe the Bible teaches that women should not serve as a pastor." That would have been an accurate statement, and I would have defended his right to say such. However, when he asserts that those who support women pastors do so not on scriptural grounds but rather because they follow the dictates of culture, he goes too far.

There are people who adamantly support women pastors on biblical grounds. I am one of them and will make what I understand to be the biblical case for women pastors.

Jesus was very radical in the way he treated women and involved women in his ministry. In order to appreciate what Jesus did, we must understand the culture in which Jesus lived.

The Jewish Culture--In Jewish law a woman was considered property rather than a person. She either belonged to her father or husband. She was not allowed to study the Law. In the synagogue women were shut apart from the men so they could not be seen. Nor could a woman actively participate in the synagogue services; she had to passively sit and listen. Nor could she teach the children in any formal manner. A woman was not required to attend the sacred feasts and festivals.

The Greek Culture--The Greeks as a whole held a low view of women. There were women priestesses in the Greek religions, but these women were most often sacred prostitutes.

Proper Greek women were confined to their quarters; they never went in public alone and never attended public assemblies. Women's purpose was essentially to serve their husbands.

Jesus' Response-- When we turn to Jesus, it is clear that he disregarded the common practice of the Jews and Greeks and extended his ministry and message to women.

Jesus, contrary to custom, talked with and taught women. He taught the Samaritan woman at the well.

John 4:27 And upon this came his disciples, and marvelled that he talked with the woman: yet no man said, What seekest thou? or, Why talkest thou with her?

Jesus talked publicly with the unclean woman who touched his cloak.

Matthew 9:20 And, behold, a woman, which was diseased with an issue of blood twelve years, came behind *him,* and touched the hem of his garment:

When he taught and fed the multitudes, women were in the crowd.

Matthew 14:13-44 When Jesus heard *of it,* he departed thence by ship into a desert place apart: and when the people had heard *thereof,* they followed him on foot out of the cities. And Jesus went forth, and saw a great multitude, and was moved with compassion toward them, and he healed their sick. And when it was evening, his disciples came to him, saying, This is a desert place, and the time is now past; send the multitude away, that they may go into the villages, and buy themselves victuals. But Jesus said unto them, They need not depart; give ye them to eat. And they say unto him, We have here but five loaves, and two fishes. He said, Bring them hither to me. And he commanded the multitude to sit down on the grass, and took the five loaves, and the two fishes, and looking up to heaven, he blessed, and brake, and gave the loaves to *his* disciples, and the disciples to the multitude. And they did all eat, and were filled: and they took up of the fragments that remained twelve baskets full. And they that had eaten were about five thousand men, beside women and children. And the apostles gathered themselves together unto Jesus, and told him all things, both what they had done, and what they had taught. And he said unto them, Come ye yourselves apart into a desert place, and rest a while: for there were many coming and going, and they had no leisure so much as to eat. And they departed into a desert place by ship privately. And the people saw them departing, and many knew him, and ran afoot thither out of all cities, and outwent them, and came together unto him. And Jesus, when he came out, saw much people, and was moved with compassion toward them, because they were as sheep not having a shepherd: and he began to teach them many things. And when the day was now far spent, his disciples came unto him, and said, This is a desert place, and now the time *is* far passed: Send them away, that they may go into the country round about, and into the villages, and buy themselves bread: for they have nothing to eat. He answered and said unto them, Give ye them to eat. And they say unto him, Shall we go and buy two hundred pennyworth of bread, and give them to eat? He saith unto them, How many loaves have ye? go and see. And when they knew, they say, Five, and two fishes. And he commanded them to make all sit down by companies upon the green grass. And they sat down in ranks, by hundreds, and by fifties. And when he had taken the five loaves and the two fishes, he looked up to heaven, and blessed, and brake the loaves, and gave *them* to his disciples to set before them; and the two fishes divided he among them all. And they did all eat, and were filled. And they took up twelve baskets full of the fragments, and of the fishes. And they that did eat of the loaves were about five thousand men.

When he healed a Canaanite woman's daughter, he talked to her in public.

Matthew 15:22 And, behold, a woman of Canaan came out of the same coasts, and cried unto him, saying, Have mercy on me, O Lord, *thou* Son of David; my daughter is grievously vexed with a devil.

He commended Mary for listening to his teaching when Martha complained that she wasn't helping with the housework.

Luke 10:38-42 Now it came to pass, as they went, that he entered into a certain village: and a certain woman named Martha received him into her house. And she had a sister called Mary, which also sat at Jesus' feet, and heard his word. But Martha was cumbered about much serving, and came to him, and said, Lord, dost thou not care that my sister hath left me to serve alone? bid her therefore that she help me. And Jesus answered and said unto her, Martha, Martha, thou art careful and troubled about many things: But one thing is needful: and Mary hath chosen that good part, which shall not be taken away from her.

Contrary to custom, Jesus allowed women to be deeply involved in his ministry. The gospels record that there were women who traveled with him to assist in his work.

The gospels do not tell us all of their names, but included in this group of women were Mary Magdalene, Joanna, Susanna, and Mary the mother of James and Joseph.

Luke 8:1-3 And it came to pass afterward, that he went throughout every city and village, preaching and shewing the glad tidings of the kingdom of God: and the twelve *were* with him, And certain women, which had been healed of evil spirits and infirmities, Mary called Magdalene, out of whom went seven devils, And Joanna the wife of Chuza Herod's steward, and Susanna, and many others, which ministered unto him of their substance.

Matthew 27:56 Among which was Mary Magdalene, and Mary the mother of James and Joses, and the mother of Zebedee's children.

Jesus broke the rule with the common treatment of women.

1. He talked in public to women.

2. He taught women about religion in public forums and private forums.

3. He gave women an active role in his ministry.

The early church, following the lead of Jesus, had women actively involved in all aspects of church life. In the book of Acts one sees a church open to women.

Women were praying with the apostles prior to Pentecost.

Acts 1:12-14 Then returned they unto Jerusalem from the mount called Olivet, which is from Jerusalem a sabbath day's journey. And when they were come in, they went up into an upper room, where abode both Peter, and James, and John, and Andrew, Philip, and Thomas, Bartholomew, and Matthew, James *the son* of Alphaeus, and Simon Zelotes, and Judas *the brother* of James. These all continued with one accord in prayer and supplication, with the women, and Mary the mother of Jesus, and with his brethren.

On the day of Pentecost Peter proclaimed the dawning of a new day in which God's spirit would empower men and women to speak and teach God's message.

Acts 2:17, 18 And it shall come to pass in the last days, saith God, I will pour out of my Spirit upon all flesh: and your sons and your daughters shall prophesy, and your young men shall see visions, and your old men shall dream dreams: And on my servants and on my handmaidens I will pour out in those days of my Spirit; and they shall prophesy:

Paul taught a group of women in Philippi.

Acts 16:13 And on the sabbath we went out of the city by a river side, where prayer was wont to be made; and we sat down, and spake unto the women which resorted *thither*.

In Berea, Paul taught women.

Acts 17:12 Therefore many of them believed; also of honourable women which were Greeks, and of men, not a few.

Priscilla was one of Apollos' teachers.

Acts 18:26 And he began to speak boldly in the synagogue: whom when Aquila and Priscilla had heard, they took him unto *them,* and expounded unto him the way of God more perfectly.

Philip had four daughters who were prophetic.

Acts 21:9 And the same man had four daughters, virgins, which did prophesy.

Paul's letters indicate women were deeply involved in his ministry. Perhaps the best example of women's involvement is in his letter to the church at Rome. In the sixteenth chapter of Romans, Paul mentions numerous women in active and prominent roles in the church. The first is Phoebe who served as a deacon in Cenchreae.

Romans 16:1, 2 I commend unto you Phebe our sister, which is a servant of the church which is at Cenchrea: That ye receive her in the Lord, as becometh saints, and that ye assist her in whatsoever business she hath need of you: for she hath been a succourer of many, and of myself also.

Priscilla is called his fellow worker.

Romans 16:3, 4 Greet Priscilla and Aquila my helpers in Christ Jesus: Who have for my life laid down their own necks: unto whom not only I give thanks, but also all the churches of the Gentiles.

Mary is mentioned as diligent worker in the church at Rome.

Romans 16:6 Greet Mary, who bestowed much labour on us.

Junia, a woman, is called an apostle.

Romans 16:7 Salute Andronicus and Junia, my kinsmen, and my fellowprisoners, who are of note among the apostles, who also were in Christ before me.

Three women—Tryphena, Tryphosa, and Persis—are mentioned as hard workers for the Lord.

Romans 16:12 Salute Tryphena and Tryphosa, who labour in the Lord. Salute the beloved Persis, which laboured much in the Lord.

In other letters of Paul, one finds references to women praying and prophesying in public worship and contending at his side for the cause of the gospel.

1Corinthians 11:5 But every woman that prayeth or prophesieth with *her* head uncovered dishonoureth her head: for that is even all one as if she were shaven.

Also, in his letter to Timothy, Paul gives instructions about women deacons (and Their Wives).

1Timothy 3:11 Even so *must their* wives *be* grave, not slanderers, sober, faithful in all things.

Coupled with these examples of women in ministry are three basic theological truths, which seem to indicate women should be involved in all aspects of the church's life.

First, There is no indication that any spiritual gift was limited to men.

1Corinthians 12:7-11 But the manifestation of the Spirit is given to every man to profit withal. For to one is given by the Spirit the word of wisdom; to another the word of knowledge by the same Spirit; To another faith by the same Spirit; to another the gifts of healing by the same Spirit; To another the working of miracles; to another prophecy; to another discerning of spirits; to another *divers* kinds of tongues; to another the interpretation of tongues: But all these worketh that one and the selfsame Spirit, dividing to every man severally as he will.

1Corinthians 14:31 For ye may all prophesy one by one, that all may learn, and all may be comforted.

1Peter 4:10 As every man hath received the gift, *even so* minister the same one to another, as good stewards of the manifold grace of God.

Second, all God's people were called his priests without any hierarchy of males.

1Peter 2:9 But ye *are* a chosen generation, a royal priesthood, an holy nation, a peculiar people; that ye should shew forth the praises of him who hath called you out of darkness into his marvellous light:

Revelations 1:6 And hath made us kings and priests unto God and his Father; to him *be* glory and dominion for ever and ever. Amen.

Revelations 5:10 And hast made us unto our God kings and priests: and we shall reign on the earth.

Third, all human distinctions were removed in Christ who united them.

Galatians 3:28 There is neither Jew nor Greek, there is neither bond nor free, there is neither male nor female: for ye are all one in Christ Jesus.

Paul believed that through faith in Jesus Christ all become God's children--one family in which those things that separated them were broken down. Now Jews and Gentiles were of the same family, the Christian master now saw the slave as an equal brother, and the man now saw the woman as an equal human being and as a sister in Christ.

What does one see happening in the early church in regard to women?

1. Women were actively involved in many areas—teachers, prophets, deacons, apostles.

2. Women were included in worship and religious instruction as

active participants.

3. The basic theology of spiritual gifts, priesthood of all believers, and oneness in Christ all moved toward the idea of women serving in an unlimited capacity in the church.

Some may begin to wonder upon what basis some people want to stop or restrict a woman from serving as a pastor.

There are two major texts that are used, and those two we must seriously examine.

1Corinthians 14:34, 35 Let your women keep silence in the churches: for it is not permitted unto them to speak; but *they are commanded* to be under obedience, as also saith the law. And if they will learn any thing, let them ask their husbands at home: for it is a shame for women to speak in the church.

This passage is hard to harmonize with the rest of the New Testament where we see women taking an active role in the church. However, this passage is even harder to harmonize with what Paul said earlier in,

1Corinthians 11:15 But if a woman have long hair, it is a glory to her: for *her* hair is given her for a covering.

Here Paul was talking about appropriate dress by Christian women so the outside world would not judge them wrongly. But the key point one needs to notice is that Paul here speaks of women praying and prophesying in worship. I do not believe that Paul is so inconsistent that within the same letter he tells women how to dress when they speak in worship and then tells women to be silent.

The best explanation is that Paul's advice here is only temporary in nature.

The thinking of this view goes along this line. Verses 34-35 are part of a larger section (1 Corinthians 14 vs. 26-40) dealing with order in church worship.

Paul was trying to bring some order back into church worship. Apparently, the women at Corinth were the main ones who were causing disorder in the church worship service. So Paul made a temporary rule for this bad situation--until the church got back on its feet functioning correctly, the women were to keep silent in worship. It is much like the governor ordering martial law on a city that has been struck by disaster. The martial law is temporary until things are restored to normal. Paul's command here is a temporary rule. The ultimate goal is to be like the rest of the churches where there were no restrictions placed upon women.

1Timothy 2:11, 12 Let the woman learn in silence with all subjection. But I suffer not a woman to teach, nor to usurp authority over the man, but to be in silence.

The question must be asked why did Paul make such a command? The rationale for this command is found in a church crisis caused by false teaching. Where Timothy was working was an area plagued by false teaching.

1Timothy 1:3-7 As I besought thee to abide still at Ephesus, when I went into Macedonia, that thou mightest charge some that they teach no other doctrine, Neither give heed to fables and endless genealogies, which minister questions, rather than godly edifying which is in faith: *so do*. Now the end of the commandment is charity out of a pure heart, and *of* a good conscience, and *of* faith unfeigned: From which some having swerved have turned aside unto vain jangling; Desiring to be teachers of the law; understanding neither what they say, nor whereof they affirm.

Paul wanted Timothy to combat these false teachers. (1 Timothy 4).

Now I believe these false teachers had made inroads into the churches through the women, especially the younger women.

1Timothy 5:11-17 But the younger widows refuse: for when they have begun to wax wanton against Christ, they will marry; Having damnation, because they have cast off their first faith. And withal they learn *to be* idle, wandering about from house to house; and not only idle, but tattlers also and busybodies, speaking things which they ought not. I will therefore that the younger women marry, bear children, guide the house, give none occasion to the adversary to speak reproachfully. For some are already turned aside after Satan. If any man or woman that believeth have widows, let them relieve them, and let not the church be charged; that it may relieve them that are widows indeed. Let the elders that rule well be counted worthy of double honour, especially they who labour in the word and doctrine.

So Paul tells these women in this church where Timothy is working to keep silent and not to teach in order to stop the spreading of the false doctrine.

Paul, evidently, wanted the women of the church where Timothy was working to keep silent because he was afraid they would deceive someone else as Eve did.

Again Paul is giving special orders to meet a bad situation. These orders were not for all churches of all times.

On the surface and out of context, this passage sounds quite clear in its restriction of women. But a different picture emerges when we consider four simple exegetical facts.

First of all, the letter of First Timothy was written to an individual, not to a church. We should expect, therefore, that the things written in the letter are related to the situation of the individual.

Secondly, vs. 3 of chapter 1 clearly states the reason for this letter to Timothy. It is not to lay down a universal system of church order.

It is to encourage and instruct him as he deals with a false teaching that is circulating among the Christians in Ephesus where he is located. This requires rightly dividing the word of truth.

2Timothy 2:15 Study to shew thyself approved unto God, a workman that needeth not to be ashamed, rightly dividing the word of truth.

The Church is in a Season of Profound of Change

1Timothy 1:3 As I besought thee to abide still at Ephesus, when I went into Macedonia, that thou mightest charge some that they teach no other doctrine,

This view is borne out by the fact that there is a change from the plural to the singular and then back to the plural in this passage.

1Timothy 2:9-12 In like manner also, that women adorn themselves in modest apparel, with shamefacedness and sobriety; not with broided hair, or gold, or pearls, or costly array; But (which becometh women professing godliness) with good works. Let the woman learn in silence with all subjection. But I suffer not a woman to teach, nor to usurp authority over the man, but to be in silence.

Afterwards, in vs. 15, he returns to quote again to the (She) instead of women.

1Timothy 2:15 Notwithstanding she shall be saved in childbearing, if they continue in faith and charity and holiness with sobriety.

This may indicate that, in writing this passage, Paul had a particular woman in mind who was primarily responsible for spreading the false teaching in Ephesus.

Be that as it may, Paul, in this passage, is obviously addressing a unique, local situation in the city of Ephesus.

So, who says women can't pastor? Not Jesus! Not Paul! And not the New Testament!

The Bible teaches that women do have an active role in every aspect of the church's life under the leadership of God's Spirit. The two times when Paul restricts women were under special circumstances – to establish order and to check the spread of heresy. Paul was trying to get sick churches back into order. Paul and the early church did not ever establish rules to limit the freedom of the Spirit's work in the lives of women. The Spirit can work in the life of any woman and lead her into any role in the church.

One student, who was obviously disturbed, challenged me with a question. "Can you show me one place in the New Testament where a woman ever functioned as a pastor?" I replied, "If you will first show me one place where a man ever functioned as a pastor!" He was stunned in that he could not think of a single example.

My answer was designed to show him how much we read into the Biblical text.

The church must recognize the Spirit's leadership and not develop rules which restrict the Spirit. People could tell me that I misinterpreted the Bible because my culture influenced me to interpret it that way. However, that sword cuts two ways. Could it be, that your culture, which has always tried to restrict women's role, causes you to interpret the Bible the way you do? Is it fair, to brand everyone who doesn't interpret the Bible the way you do as someone who no longer believes the Bible? Are you always perfect in your understanding of Scripture? As far as I'm concerned women are to hold any position a man can hold.

Don't forget the young generation Timothy said "let no one despise thy youth."

Chapter Twenty
The Transforming Fire of God's Power

One thing I've heard the Church cry out for is the Fire of God. The Fire of God burns all the impurities out and transforms lives. I am overwhelmed with the dynamite of God's transforming power that works in people's lives when they surrender themselves to the One who existed before the universe was spoken into existence. We really need to become that Prototype Church and the only way is through being fully transformed by the Fire of God.

Tell the Lord Jesus that you're through with trying to run your own life. Tell Him that you believe He came to this earth as the Son of God and took the punishment for your sins when He died on the cross.

John 14:6 Jesus saith unto him, I am the way, the truth, and the life: no man cometh unto the Father, but by me.

So, for God to become our Father, not just our Creator, we must have a personal encounter with the Lord Jesus. The amazing dynamite of God's transforming power to change us from self-focused people into God-and-other-people focused people is something that only comes through letting the living Lord Jesus become the center of our lives.

Now, let us look at the fire of God's power to overcome the powers of darkness.

1John 4:4 Ye are of God, little children, and have overcome them: because greater is he that is in you, than he that is in the world.

So we shouldn't be surprised at hearing stories of great triumphs over the devil. Remember, our Commander-in-Chief has never lost a battle. He's El Shaddai, God Almighty.

God has the time of His life doing it. It's one of His favorite things. Check it out in Second Chronicles 16:9. What a fantastic God!

2Chronicles 16:9 For the eyes of the LORD run to and fro throughout the whole earth, to shew himself strong in the behalf of *them* whose heart *is* perfect toward him. Herein thou hast done foolishly: therefore from henceforth thou shalt have wars.

He never runs out of ideas of how to show up in the most horrendous and seemingly hopeless situations because He's ingenious in His creativity. He has at least millions of ways of demonstrating the fire of His power that we've never heard of or thought of. So, why don't we wise up and give Him more opportunities to put Himself on display?

Matthew 16:18 And I say also unto thee, That thou art Peter, and upon this rock I will build my church; and the gates of hell shall not prevail against it.

We must only and always be impressed with the One who said these words—never the one who challenges them.

I can imagine some people questioning the validity of linking the fire of God in purifying with His tender love. I can imagine others wanting to avoid hearing this because we all know that getting too close to fire is very painful, and many are in enough pain now. I've had people tell me the messages were too convicting. Obviously, between their initial reaction and these conversations they had decided to try me out again.

My heart longs for believers everywhere to understand that when we see our heavenly Bridegroom face to face, we'll see that

His eyes not only burn with awesome holiness and shine with immaculate purity, but they blaze with deep love for us. It's all about being prepared to become the Bride of Christ at the marriage supper of the Lamb. It's about preparation for the big long-haul of time called eternity.

Ephesians 5:25-27 Husbands, love your wives, even as Christ also loved the church, and gave himself for it; That he might sanctify and cleanse it with the washing of water by the word, That he might present it to himself a glorious church, not having spot, or wrinkle, or any such thing; but that it should be holy and without blemish.

Now let's see how the tender, strongly ambitious love of God manifests itself, or Himself, in relation to purifying us. Sin in any form is the most destructive force to the well-being of our minds, bodies, souls, and spirits.

Romans 6:23 For the wages of sin *is* death; but the gift of God *is* eternal life through Jesus Christ our Lord.

It is like a disease. Let's take cancer as an example. Ultimately, it is destructive if not removed. We realize when we go to the doctors for tests that they help us by giving us a correct diagnosis. Our very life can depend on it. When we realize we have the disease, we desperately want to be rid of it. Wouldn't it be ridiculous to either avoid the doctor's ability to give us an accurate diagnosis of the disease, or resent them when they do; worse still, if we would do nothing about having it removed in the many ways that God has provided. It could be through medical science or a miracle healing directly through prayer, or through applying natural means, or a combination of any of these ways. Following this analogy we can only conclude that God does us the greatest favor by convicting us of this most destructive force called sin. When we realize that He is equally motivated by His love and His holiness to bring conviction, we see it as one of the greatest ways He can bless us.

Revelations 3:18, 19 I counsel thee to buy of me gold tried in the fire, that thou mayest be rich; and white raiment, that thou mayest be clothed, and *that* the shame of thy nakedness do not appear; and anoint thine eyes with eyesalve, that thou mayest see. As many as I love, I rebuke and chasten: be zealous therefore, and repent.

Revelations 3:11, 12 Behold, I come quickly: hold that fast which thou hast, that no man take thy crown. Him that overcometh will I make a pillar in the temple of my God, and he shall go no more out: and I will write upon him the name of my God, and the name of the city of my God, *which is* new Jerusalem, which cometh down out of heaven from my God: and *I will write upon him* my new name.

This fire of the Holy Spirit was to burn out the things in my life that were un-Christlike. Many times, I would either be convicted directly by the Holy Spirit over something in my life that was grieving Him, or God would cause others to correct me. It was a very painful but necessary experience in my spiritual growth. I didn't have the full understanding at that time that it was an act of God's love to bless me. But I was beginning to understand that the depth of our worship to the One True God, the Father, Son, and Holy Spirit is in direct proportion to the revelation we have of His holiness.

2Corinthians 7:1 Having therefore these promises, dearly beloved, let us cleanse ourselves from all filthiness of the flesh and spirit, perfecting holiness in the fear of God.

An effective way I have found of obeying this order is to ask God to show me my heart as only He sees it.

2Chronicles 6:30 Then hear thou from heaven thy dwelling place, and forgive, and render unto every man according unto all his ways, whose heart thou knowest; (for thou only knowest the hearts of the children of men:)

The two root sins from which all other sins come are unbelief and pride. They are the two sins by which satan tempted Eve in the Garden of Eden.

Genesis 3:1 Now the serpent was more subtil than any beast of the field which the LORD God had made. And he said unto the woman, Yea, hath God said, Ye shall not eat of every tree of the garden?

Genesis 3:5 For God doth know that in the day ye eat thereof, then your eyes shall be opened, and ye shall be as gods, knowing good and evil.

Proverbs 8:13 The fear of the LORD *is* to hate evil: pride, and arrogancy, and the evil way, and the froward mouth, do I hate.

Simply put, it means to have a passion for holiness in thought, word, and deed and to hate sin in the same dimensions. The Word of God alone is the standard.

I also learned that true brokenness before God and man is a powerful means of releasing the power of the Holy Spirit upon us.

Isaiah 66:2 For all those *things* hath mine hand made, and all those *things* have been, saith the LORD: but to this *man* will I look, *even* to *him that is* poor and of a contrite spirit, and trembleth at my word.

I was also greatly encouraged by noticing that the enabling power of the Holy Spirit to minister to others was in exact proportion to the level of purity I was experiencing. Purity and power became the same.

Leviticus 10:3 Then Moses said unto Aaron, This *is it* that the LORD spake, saying, I will be sanctified in them that come nigh me, and before all the people I will be glorified. And Aaron held his peace.

It is only through God's Love that He brings us through deep conviction of sin. These experiences draw me much closer to Him and deepened my love for Him and understanding of Him.

Matthew 5:8 Blessed *are* the pure in heart: for they shall see God.

Never resist the convicting fires of the Holy Spirit; embrace them and cooperate with God in true repentance, with gratitude that He is bringing you closer in relationship with Jesus and preparing you for greater usefulness in His Kingdom purposes.

Now let's take a look at God giving us another invitation to become more like Him by further cooperating with the fires of His love, and to avoid the fire of His judgment.

Jeremiah 4:3, 4 For thus saith the LORD to the men of Judah and Jerusalem, Break up your fallow ground, and sow not among thorns. Circumcise yourselves to the LORD, and take away the foreskins of your heart, ye men of Judah and inhabitants of Jerusalem: lest my fury come forth like fire, and burn that none can quench *it*, because of the evil of your doings.

Plowing involves disruption of the status quo and uncomfortable change.

John 8:32 And ye shall know the truth, and the truth shall make you free.

The truth often hurts before we experience the freedom.

Let's look at some of the agricultural reasons for plowing and then apply them spiritually so that we can obey God's injunctions here. The first purpose for plowing is to get rid of the hardness of the soil. We can too easily develop a coldness of heart toward God, His people, or the unconverted. Therefore we need to maintain a vigilant watch over the condition of our hearts. When we are really serious about having a spiritual heart transplant, we'll cry out to God with intensity and faith for the Holy Spirit to break our hearts over what breaks God's heart. We may have to have the supernatural revelation of our heart's condition as only God knows it before a permanent change takes place.

John 17:9 I pray for them: I pray not for the world, but for them which thou hast given me; for they are thine.

2Chronicles 6:30 Then hear thou from heaven thy dwelling place, and forgive, and render unto every man according unto all his ways, whose heart thou knowest; (for thou only knowest the hearts of the children of men:)

Another purpose for plowing is that the stones and weeds can be removed. I always mention in my meetings that when the rain of

God comes the rocks rise to the surface. The stones represent hindrances to spiritual progress, like wrong priorities. We need to have a continual check in that area of our lives and make the necessary adjustments.

1. Our responses to God's Word determine our goals.
2. Our goals determine our choices.
3. Our choices determine our character.
4. Our character determines our priorities.
5. Our priorities determine our destinies.

It is crucial that we understand what our priorities are from God's Word. Genuine Christianity flows out of a love relationship with the Lord Jesus.

Ephesians 5:18 And be not drunk with wine, wherein is excess; but be filled with the Spirit;

And the daily infilling of the Holy Spirit, as we ask for it equips us to do His will in the following four areas of major importance:

1. **Worship** and praise, and seeking His face and presence

Psalms 34:1 *A Psalm* of David, when he changed his behaviour before Abimelech; who drove him away, and he departed. I will bless the LORD at all times: his praise *shall* continually *be* in my mouth.

Psalms 27:8 *When thou saidst,* Seek ye my face; my heart said unto thee, Thy face, LORD, will I seek.

Psalms 105:4 Seek the LORD, and his strength: seek his face evermore.

2. Time in God's **Word** getting to know Him and His ways

Jeremiah 9:23, 24 Thus saith the LORD, Let not the wise *man* glory in his wisdom, neither let the mighty *man* glory in his might, let not the rich *man* glory in his riches: But let him that glorieth glory in this, that he understandeth and knoweth me, that I *am* the LORD which exercise lovingkindness, judgment, and righteousness, in the earth: for in these *things* I delight, saith the LORD.

Psalms 25:4 Shew me thy ways, O LORD; teach me thy paths.

3. **Waiting** on God:

Making sure our hearts are clean from any undealt with sin.

Psalms 66:18 If I regard iniquity in my heart, the Lord will not hear *me:*

When there's a breakdown in any of these areas of our lives, we know that we have need for serious "plowing" to remove the boulders and stones that hinder the fulfillment of our destinies.

Let me ask you a question, what things need to be removed in order to make time for God's priorities? Your destiny depends on it. And that's serious stuff. The good is always the enemy of the best. It's also important to know what our main ministry functions are so that we keep within those parameters, and do not get sidetracked by the pressure from other people's requests and expectations or demands. The weeds come as a result of neglect. We need to repent of the sins of omission.

James 4:17 Therefore to him that knoweth to do good, and doeth *it* not, to him it is sin.

Remember, delayed obedience, partial obedience, and obedience with murmuring is all disobedience according to God's Word. Disobedience represents a serious obstruction from weeds that need to be plowed out.

Psalms 119:75 I know, O LORD, that thy judgments *are* right, and *that* thou in faithfulness hast afflicted me.

We do ourselves the greatest favor when we get the message and take God seriously. Don't you think it's kind of dumb to do anything else? Let's wise up, because the alternative is always grim.

Another purpose for plowing is so that new seeds can be planted. In the parable of the sower sowing his seed, Jesus clearly teaches us in Luke 8:11 that the seed is an illustration of the Word of God.

Luke 8:11 Now the parable is this: The seed is the word of God.

We need to be seeking God expectantly, as a way of life for direct, fresh revelation of truth as we daily read His Word, so that we can walk in it. As we repent of everything that displeases Him, and walk in the light of God's truth, He encourages us from His Word that He will reveal more truth to us.

Psalms 36:9 For with thee *is* the fountain of life: in thy light shall we see light.

We should never be content with only receiving secondhand revelation of truth. Jesus promised that the Holy Spirit would come and teach us all things.

By the way, disobedience is one of the greatest hindrances to revelation of truth. Why should God reveal more truth to us if we're not obedient to already revealed truth?

Another purpose for plowing is so that the rain can be received in deeper dimensions. How we need to stir ourselves up and commit to prioritizing prayer for genuine revival and spiritual awakening so that the rain of the Spirit can drench our lives, our churches, our cities, our nations.

Zechariah 10:1 Ask ye of the LORD rain in the time of the latter rain; *so* the LORD shall make bright clouds, and give them showers of rain, to every one grass in the field.

In genuine revival God does more to extend His Kingdom in minutes, than what takes place in weeks, months, or years of God-ordained Christian activity. When that truth grips your heart, you don't need others to call you and prompt you to intercede for revival. You not only do so as a way of life, but you call others to do so. Revival of the Church and spiritual awakening among the lost is the only answer to the desperate need of this hour and age. God promises us results to our desperate, persevering cries, from humble, clean, loving hearts.

Isaiah 59:19 So shall they fear the name of the LORD from the west, and his glory from the rising of the sun. When the enemy shall come in like a flood, the Spirit of the LORD shall lift up a standard against him.

Isaiah 52:10 The LORD hath made bare his holy arm in the eyes of all the nations; and all the ends of the earth shall see the salvation of our God.

The final purpose for plowing is that a more bountiful harvest can be reaped. As we cry out to God to give us a far greater spiritual ambition to be used by Him in this end-time harvest, He will answer us. He's not looking for clever people, but clean people. He's not looking for talented people, but available people. He's not looking for people-pleasers, but for God-fearing people. He's not looking for self-assured people, but on God dependent-only people, people who have a passion for God and His glory. He's not looking for people who can write a thesis on evangelism. He's looking for people with a burdened heart for the lost who will go out to where they are, love them, pray for them, weep for them, witness to them and be involved with their lives, and give their lives for the lost if necessary.

Joel 3:13, 14 Put ye in the sickle, for the harvest is ripe: come, get you down; for the press is full, the fats overflow; for their wickedness *is* great. Multitudes, multitudes in the valley of decision: for the day of the LORD *is* near in the valley of decision.

It's harvest time all over the world. That means that God has heard the cries of those of us who have been praying for the lost in every nation of the world, naming each nation separately, for numbers of decades. We've asked God to prepare the hearts of the unconverted in every nation so that when they hear the gospel they will immediately respond. We've asked God to reveal Himself in visions and dreams to the lost who have never heard the gospel. We've asked God to direct them to Christians who will explain to them the message of salvation and give them a Bible. It's happening. It's happening in every nation. It's harvest time. We either are involved as a way of life in witnessing and winning people to Jesus and are therefore followers of Him, or we are disobedient and don't qualify to be a follower.

Matthew 4:19 And he saith unto them, Follow me, and I will make you fishers of men.

I don't know of anything in life that produces hardness of heart like the sin of resentment to those who have wronged us. We are such fragile beings. And we live in a fallen world where we seem to have the unique capacity of hurting each other whether out of our own humanness or through our all too frequent misunderstanding of each other. The reality is that in this life we are going to get hurt to some degree or another. The greater the hurt, the deeper the pain. The deeper the pain, the more tempted we are to yield to the force of resentment to the perpetrator of the pain.

Without the stronger healing force of forgiveness we become subject to the utter bondage, the slavery, the destructive force of unforgiveness.

It is important for us to understand that the purposes of the fire of God's love in our lives are often parallel to the purposes of natural fire. Natural fire melts hard substances. The Lord yearns for us to believe that He alone knows the extent of our hurt and pain because there is nothing hidden from His sight.

Psalms 147:5 Great *is* our Lord, and of great power: his understanding *is* infinite.

Psalms 147:3 He healeth the broken in heart, and bindeth up their wounds.

Psalms 22:19 But be not thou far from me, O LORD: O my strength, haste thee to help me.

It is perfectly possible, in our ignorance, to have resentment toward God.

Deuteronomy 32:4 *He is* the Rock, his work *is* perfect: for all his ways *are* judgment: a God of truth and without iniquity, just and right *is* he.

Let's look at some reasons for feeling hurt, where we could be tempted to wrongly judge people:

1. We were not consulted before a decision was made. Perhaps we were not meant to be involved in that responsibility.

2. We were not told about something for which we should have been informed. Maybe the breakdown of communication was with someone else who had been delegated to do so and had failed.

3. We were not given the attention we requested from an individual or insufficient attention for our liking. It could be, that for a number of reasons our receiving attention was not a legitimate priority for that individual at that time, or their amount of availability was equally limited.

4. We were not given the recognition for our labors that we thought we deserved. Perhaps God overruled the recognition by withholding it in order to test the motivation of our hearts. Jesus said, "*I do not receive praise from men*," simply because He gave all the glory to the Father.

5. We were corrected by someone where we considered the judgment to be unfair. Maybe we were immediately defensive and didn't have the humility to ask God to show us if there was even a small percentage of truth in their overall judgment.

6. We were seemingly ignored by someone when we were in the presence of others. It's absolutely possible that the person either didn't see us, or never heard us, or for any number of reasons wasn't able to speak or respond to us. For example, it could be

because of the pressures of responsibilities on the person, or their physical condition, or because they were under great stress, to name a few.

7. We were not included in a group situation where we thought we should have been. It could be that there was an unexplainable oversight, or perhaps the group felt it would be wiser and more beneficial for all concerned, including ourselves, if we were not included.

We need to honestly ask the Holy Spirit to show us where our ego and pride may have been the cause of our pain when we're feeling offended. When we really come to the place of death to that monster called self and want it to be crucified, we enter into real freedom.

You can't offend a dead man. On the other hand, there are times when others have totally distorted our characters through what they've said about us, or have perpetuated lies about us. God understands the pain that comes from those experiences.

If we will forgive them, He will heal us and vindicate us in His way and time.

Isaiah 54:17 No weapon that is formed against thee shall prosper; and every tongue *that* shall rise against thee in judgment thou shalt condemn. This *is* the heritage of the servants of the LORD, and their righteousness *is* of me, saith the LORD.

We also need to be far more sensitive in all our communications with each other. Here's a check list:

1. Is the communication really necessary?

2. Is it our responsibility to communicate, or another's?

3. Are we communicating in the right timing?

4. Have we the right method of communicating?

5. Are we in the right attitude of heart? Have we checked our motives?

6. Are we prepared to speak only 100 percent truth in humility, gentleness, love, and graciousness?

Luke 12:48 But he that knew not, and did commit things worthy of stripes, shall be beaten with few *stripes*. For unto whomsoever much is given, of him shall be much required: and to whom men have committed much, of him they will ask the more.

We need to be especially sensitive to everything related to our communications with spiritual leaders. They are subject to a great deal of unnecessary stress by virtue of their high profile, from people who, often in ignorance, create that stress. Let's heed this admonition so that it can be avoided. If we have wrongly judged others, God requires repentance of that sin.

Matthew 7:1, 2 Judge not, that ye be not judged. For with what judgment ye judge, ye shall be judged: and with what measure ye mete, it shall be measured to you again.

Only repentance will release us from God's judgment that is already on us. If we have shared our wrong judgment with others, we will also need to make restitution by telling them.

How much disunity in the Body of Christ would be avoided if only we would live by the Word of God?

Matthew 5:23, 24 Therefore if thou bring thy gift to the altar, and there rememberest that thy brother hath ought against thee;

Leave there thy gift before the altar, and go thy way; first be reconciled to thy brother, and then come and offer thy gift.

If someone has sinned against us, we're to go to him or her *alone* and express our forgiveness and do everything we know to be reconciled.

Matthew 18:15 Moreover if thy brother shall trespass against thee, go and tell him his fault between thee and him alone: if he shall hear thee, thou hast gained thy brother.

Unity in Christ's Body of believers is the most powerful influence for unbelievers to be convinced that the Lord Jesus is the Son of God and that God loves His disciples as He loved His Son. What an incredible impact! That's why forgiveness is so essential for world evangelization.

John 17:23 I in them, and thou in me, that they may be made perfect in one; and that the world may know that thou hast sent me, and hast loved them, as thou hast loved me.

Hebrews 12:15 Looking diligently lest any man fail of the grace of God; lest any root of bitterness springing up trouble *you,* and thereby many be defiled;

Obviously, from this Scripture there is enough of God's grace available to enable anyone to forgive an offense. The following scriptural principles, when put into practice, will release anyone into the full freedom of forgiveness. They have been tried and proven true.

1. Realize that forgiveness is an act of the will. We have to want to forgive. Some people simply don't want to. They prefer to harbor their resentment and continue in their bondage.

2. Understand that resentment is destructive to the mind, body, soul, and spirit.

Proverbs 14:30 A sound heart *is* the life of the flesh: but envy the rottenness of the bones.

3. Realize that we will not be forgiven by God unless we forgive those who have hurt us.

Mark 11:25 And when ye stand praying, forgive, if ye have ought against any: that your Father also which is in heaven may forgive you your trespasses.

That's heavy! Is there anyone who doesn't need God's ongoing forgiveness?

4. Think of all that God has forgiven us for.

Ephesians 4:32 And be ye kind one to another, tenderhearted, forgiving one another, even as God for Christ's sake hath forgiven you.

Colossians 3:13 Forbearing one another, and forgiving one another, if any man have a quarrel against any: even as Christ forgave you, so also *do* ye.

God forgives us instantly, joyfully, and wholly.

5. Thank the Lord for any or all of the blessings He has brought to us through the people who have hurt us. Write them down. Thankfulness and resentment have a hard time remaining together.

6. Think of the needs—mental, physical, emotional, and spiritual—of the individuals at the time of their hurting us. Their needs then—and now—are probably greater than ours.

7. We ask God to give us His supernatural ability to love and forgive those people. Acknowledge that this is the work of the Holy Spirit and receive it by faith.

Romans 5:5 And hope maketh not ashamed; because the love of God is shed abroad in our hearts by the Holy Ghost which is given unto us.

Hebrews 11:6 But without faith *it is* impossible to please *him:* for he that cometh to God must believe that he is, and *that* he is a rewarder of them that diligently seek him.

Galatians 5:6 For in Jesus Christ neither circumcision availeth any thing, nor uncircumcision; but faith which worketh by love.

1Corinthians 13:8 Charity never faileth: but whether *there be* prophecies, they shall fail; whether *there be* tongues, they shall cease; whether *there be* knowledge, it shall vanish away.

8. We ask God for opportunities to express His love to these people both in word and in deed.

1John 3:17, 18 But whoso hath this world's good, and seeth his brother have need, and shutteth up his bowels *of compassion* from him, how dwelleth the love of God in him? My little children, let us not love in word, neither in tongue; but in deed and in truth.

Benevolent acts and expressed love make it terribly hard for resentment to exist. They suffocate it.

9. Become a regular intercessor for them. Pray only for God to bless them, encourage them, comfort them, strengthen them, and meet their deepest needs.

Matthew 5:44 But I say unto you, Love your enemies, bless them that curse you, do good to them that hate you, and pray for them which despitefully use you, and persecute you;

As we persist in these spiritual exercises we find we are being conformed into the image of the Lord Jesus, and after all, that's our goal; so that makes us express gratitude to God for allowing the painful circumstances in the first place. And we've again proved that His matchless grace has brought us through. What a God!

The deeper we love people the more we will suffer when hurt by them, particularly where injustice is involved. Therefore, the ones we need to forgive the most are often those closest to us in relationships.

Let us check through the list for any hidden resentments: wives, husbands, fathers, mothers, friends, schoolteachers, spiritual leaders, people we've been teamed with in ministries, people with whom we work, people over us in authority, people under our authority, politicians and government officials from our own nation or other nations, governments that have hurt those who are close to us, and any other categories you know of.

Unfortunately there are times when, in their human frailty, spiritual leaders misjudge us. The greatest saints who have ever lived have all had fragile feet, so don't expect perfection. Often leaders, because of the weight of their many responsibilities, react too quickly and make wrong judgments of others.

We need to learn from Hannah in First Samuel 1, how to pass this kind of difficult test if we are the one who is hurt. Eli the priest totally misjudged the godly woman Hannah, in the temple, when she was fasting and quietly pouring out her anguished heart to the Lord in prayer.

Eli accused her of drunkenness and rebuked her. How painful; how unjust.

The very person who should have been the one to minister comfort, understanding, and encouragement to her in her hour of need, was an instrument of great pain.

Hannah's name means "grace" and this beautiful quality of the Holy Spirit was evident when she respectfully addressed him and gently explained what she was doing. Immediately, Eli prophesied a blessing from God over her, telling her that her prayers were heard and fulfillment was on the way. Obviously Hannah knew that she needed to instantly forgive her spiritual leader to have favor with God. By doing so, God was able to release the word of the Lord through Eli to bless her.

If we hold resentment in our hearts to spiritual leaders who have hurt us, we will not be able to receive the many blessings through them that God has planned to give us. Thank God that His mercy is always extended to a truly repentant heart. Now let's learn from a spiritual leader who failed to forgive a person under his authority.

As we carefully read through the events of the story in Second Samuel 13, of Absalom murdering his brother Amnon, we find in verses 37-39 that Absalom then fled and went to another city for three years. David mourned for him every day and longed to go to him. But David, as his leader, never confronted Absalom, or disciplined him, or sought for reconciliation with him. Joab, David's military leader, and a wise woman from the city of Tekoa were both used by God to get the message through to David that he needed to invite Absalom back home. If David had forgiven his son, he wouldn't have needed all that input. Then, when Absalom did return home it was on the condition that Absalom was not to see David's face.

2Samuel 14:24 And the king said, Let him turn to his own house, and let him not see my face. So Absalom returned to his own house, and saw not the king's face.

In verse 28 we're told that Absalom was in Jerusalem for two full years but did not see the king's face. After that, Absalom tried on two occasions to get Joab to go to King David on his behalf, to try to get permission for Absalom to see his father.

2Samuel 14:33 So Joab came to the king, and told him: and when he had called for Absalom, he came to the king, and bowed himself on his face to the ground before the king: and the king kissed Absalom.

Superficially it looks as if everything is okay. But it's not. There's not a word written about any communication, reconciliation, or fellowship. And without fellowship of some kind there's no restoration of relationship. Conversely, forgiveness will always lead to fellowship.

2Samuel 15:1 And it came to pass after this, that Absalom prepared him chariots and horses, and fifty men to run before him.

It was the start of Absalom's schemes of winning the hearts of the people to himself, which finally ended in open revolt and betrayal. I believe that David's lack of forgiveness became a cause of temptation to Absalom to betray his father.

In Matthew 18:7 Jesus gives us a solemn warning about being a cause of temptation to others:

Matthew 18:7 Woe unto the world because of offences! for it must needs be that offences come; but woe to that man by whom the offence cometh!

James 3:1 My brethren, be not many masters, knowing that we shall receive the greater condemnation.

David's lack of forgiveness brought not only God's disapproval on his life, but further great suffering to the people he led. And that's another long story, which is told in the ensuing chapters of Second Samuel. To conclude this on the fire of God's love to purify us, I want you to know there is no way you can avoid the Fire of God if you want to be a part of this Prototype Church.

Chapter Twenty One
Christ Centered Prototype Church

One thing we must all believe and fully receive is the resurrection of Jesus Christ.

Romans 10:10 For with the heart man believeth unto righteousness; and with the mouth confession is made unto salvation.

We believe in the doctrine of the resurrection, but if we really believed in the resurrection in our hearts, our lives would be radically different. How would they be different? First, we would not be so consumed with the things that are temporary, but rather with the things that are eternal. There is a saying that some are "so heavenly minded that they are not earthly good," but the truth is that many Christians are so earthly minded that they are not doing much good for heaven or earth. The historic truth is that those who were the most heavenly minded are the ones who have always done the most good for this present world.

Those who are heavenly minded, who are obeying the exhortation to seek first the kingdom, are the freest people on the earth, and they will become more and more obvious in the times to come.

Colossians 3:1-4 If ye then be risen with Christ, seek those things which are above, where Christ sitteth on the right hand of God. Set your affection on things above, not on things on the earth. For ye are dead, and your life is hid with Christ in God. When Christ, *who is* our life, shall appear, then shall ye also appear with him in glory.

The resurrection is the greatest hope that even the worst thing that could ever happen will result as a victory.

2Corinthians 2:14 Now thanks *be* unto God, which always causeth us to triumph in Christ, and maketh manifest the savour of his knowledge by us in every place.

So for those who follow Him, it is not a matter of *if* they will have victory, but *how*. If we follow Christ, we cannot lose. Just as the most celebrated victories in war or sports are those that are won against the greatest odds, the same is true in Christ. We want to see the supernatural power of God, but we just don't want to be put in a place where we must have it. We want to see the great victories, but we don't want to find ourselves in the place where we must have them. We are in the times when we must, so let's embrace the opportunities.

Even the great heroes of The Bible grew in the faith until they could be used this way. David fought with the lion and bear before he faced Goliath. The same is true with us. He may one day lead us into a great and historic conflict and victory, but we must not miss the little ones today that are intended to prepare us for what is to come.

Rejoice in every victory regardless of how big or small. Embrace every trial regardless of how big or small. If we are following Christ, it is impossible for us to not experience victory in everything—that is the only way He will ever lead us. Even so, as the Scripture reads above, it is **"triumph in Christ,"** not just ours.

What did His triumph look like?

The greatest victory there will ever be was the cross. However, it did not look like a victory. When Jesus was nailed to the cross, it looked like evil had prevailed against the greatest Good to ever walk the earth, but what looked like the greatest defeat was the greatest victory. So great victories may not always look like great victories at first. We cannot give up hope regardless of how it may look like evil has prevailed. Evil may appear to win for a time, but it cannot last.

The ultimate victory of Christ is sure and it is for eternity. Those who believe in their hearts in the resurrection are freed from the ultimate fear, and therefore they will be the most free and happy people on the earth. As we come to believe in our hearts that Christ always leads us in His triumph, that in everything there will be ultimate victory, then how can we fail to face every battle with courage?

Romans 8:28 And we know that all things work together for good to them that love God, to them who are the called according to *his* purpose.

James 1:2-4 My brethren, count it all joy when ye fall into divers temptations; Knowing *this,* that the trying of your faith worketh patience. But let patience have *her* perfect work, that ye may be perfect and entire, wanting nothing.

The "perfect and complete, lacking in nothing" that he speaks of here is Christ-likeness. Everything in our lives is intended to bring forth the nature of Christ in us, and by this one thing we can understand all things.

Romans 8:28, 29 And we know that all things work together for good to them that love God, to them who are the called according to *his* purpose. For whom he did foreknow, he also did predestinate *to be* conformed to the image of his Son, that he might be the firstborn among many brethren.

We are called to be heirs of God in Christ. There is no higher calling in all of creation. Everything happening in our lives is intended to prepare us for this high calling by working in us Christ's nature. Christ is the answer to every human problem, and He is the answer to every problem we're now facing. It is not just that He has the answers, but He *is* the answer. If we are living in the knowledge that the One we serve is over all rule and authority and dominion, how can we fear? Every challenge is an opportunity to grow in faith, so a key to the victorious life is to not waste our trials.

Romans 14:17 For the kingdom of God is not meat and drink; but righteousness, and peace, and joy in the Holy Ghost.

If we are doing what is right in the sight of the Lord, we will know a peace and joy that is greater than can ever be known in any other way. As the troubles, fears, and darkness in the world increase, those who are living in the kingdom will stand out even more because of their peace and joy. Peace and joy will be one of the greatest signs that one is a true citizen of the kingdom in the times to come. How can we fail to have peace and joy when we know and follow the King of kings who sits above all rule and authority and dominion and whose kingdom is surely coming?

Isaiah 9:7 Of the increase of *his* government and peace *there shall be* no end, upon the throne of David, and upon his kingdom, to order it, and to establish it with judgment and with justice from henceforth even for ever. The zeal of the LORD of hosts will perform this.

Invest in the kingdom and your investment will forever increase. Those who seek His kingdom first will be increasing in the peace and joy of His kingdom.

Proverbs 4:18 But the path of the just *is* as the shining light, that shineth more and more unto the perfect day.

The normal Christian life is one that gets brighter and brighter. Regardless of how dark things may become in this world, we have a different reality that is getting ever brighter. The times in the world will get darker, but this world is not our reality.

Isaiah 60:1, 2 Arise, shine; for thy light is come, and the glory of the LORD is risen upon thee. For, behold, the darkness shall cover the earth, and gross darkness the people: but the LORD shall arise upon thee, and his glory shall be seen upon thee.

The time of the greatest darkness in this world will be the time when we will see His glory on us.

Isaiah 60:3 And the Gentiles shall come to thy light, and kings to the brightness of thy rising.

It is darkest just before dawn, and it is getting darker for a time, but this will only make the glory brighter when it is revealed on God's people.

The fear of death is the ultimate fear, so once this fear is overcome by the assurance of the resurrection, breaking the yoke of any other fear will be easy. This is why the celebration and remembrance of the resurrection is so crucial to the Christian life. As we abide in the knowledge of this truth, we can more easily overcome any other fear.

The devil uses fear to oppress and control. In Christ, we walk by faith not by fear. Fear is fundamentally a device of Satan, and those who let fear control them are serving him more than Christ regardless of what they may say.

Rev 21:8 But the fearful, and unbelieving, and the abominable, and murderers, and whoremongers, and sorcerers, and idolaters, and all liars, shall have their part in the lake which burneth with fire and brimstone: which is the second death.

Here we see that the cowardly is listed before the abominable, murderers, immoral, sorcerers, idolaters, and liars. The fact is that those who are led by fear, so as to be cowardly, are not Christ's.

Revelations 20:14, 15 And death and hell were cast into the lake of fire. This is the second death. And whosoever was not found written in the book of life was cast into the lake of fire.

Those who truly believe will be courageous, and they will not be controlled by fear. There is no place for cowardice in Christianity. In this way, those who truly believe in Him will soon be distinguished. Let us resolve now that fear will not control us, but we will live by faith in the risen Son of God. We are called to be dead to this world, and what can be done to a dead man? A dead man does not have fears of failure, or rejection, or any other fear. If we have died with Christ, we can now walk in the power of His resurrection and should have no fear.

The prophets of old desired to see the times that we have been privileged to live in. Those who have dreamed of the time when we get to meet and talk to the great heroes of the faith will be shocked to see that they were even more longing for of talking to the saints who lived in these times. The greatest faith and the greatest exploits will soon be demonstrated by those who have not wasted their trials, and therefore will not waste this greatest of opportunities to walk with God.

Many things will shake in 2013, but we have a kingdom that cannot be shaken, and all that is being shaken is in order to reveal the kingdom. Build your life on what can never be shaken, and the hope that can never disappoint us. Resolve that you will live in faith in the resurrection. Those who believe shall do great exploits.

The Church is in a Season of Profound of Change

CHAPTER TWENTY TWO
The Anointed Eagles

During the Waves of Revival in Belleville, IL God released a vision that was most powerful. I am going to attempt to give you the full picture here. I pray that your eyes are open to see in the Spirit.

Exodus 19:4 Ye have seen what I did unto the Egyptians, and *how* I bare you on eagles' wings, and brought you unto myself.

I have found myself lately revisiting a Trance vision that I had. Perhaps we are moving into the season where it will have significance and application among us. This has to do with the New Prototype Church coming forth.

I remember going very deep into the realm of the Spirit. My body was stationary, but my spirit was moving forward on a journey toward something beautiful. The first thing I saw was a crystal clear river flowing from a huge throne in the distance. The throne was so large it appeared to have many levels.

The river was very deep and flowing swiftly. I knew somehow that, in these waters, there was deliverance, freedom, and full provision for all that would be needed by the bride in the last days. There was a tangible anointing and glory released by the swirling of the water.

I then saw an eagle flying in from the west and I knew he was coming with a message. An eagle often types the prophet or prophetic seer anointing. I discerned that this eagle was bringing a word of revelation for the bride. As I watched, a white dove flying in over the churning waters joined the eagle. The dove flew faster and faster, following the eagle.

A voice explained that the dove represented a true and genuine baptism of the Holy Ghost.

I understood that the deep waters beckoning the bride represented the profound revelations and mysteries that the bride of Christ had been called to walk in. God's Word is being revealed to her in more intimate ways as the waters coursed over her. As I looked up again I saw the eagle beginning to circle a large blue ball. I could see the shapes of the continents and realized that I was seeing the earth. As the eagle continued to circle the globe, the white dove was following closely behind. Suddenly there appeared another bird, also white in color but much larger than the dove. It had the same body structure as the eagle but his feathers were pure white. Loudly I exclaimed, "It's a white eagle."

Then an angel stepped into view dressed in white. I discerned that he was not an ordinary angel but carried a high level of authority.

I need to explain a bit about the nature of these trance visions. I am sometimes able to communicate with those in the room while not breaking free from the spiritual realm.

The angel then asked me if I was familiar with this white eagle. The angel explained that it was more important for now that I see and hear him than understand him. The angel then began to teach me with the patience and simplicity one would use in interacting with a small child, carefully repeating the details of what I had seen thus far. He reminded me that first the eagle came leading the dove, a type of the prophet leading the way for the true infilling of the Holy Spirit.

Ephesians 1:13, 14 In whom ye also *trusted*, after that ye heard the word of truth, the gospel of your salvation: in whom also after that ye believed, ye were sealed with that holy Spirit of promise, Which is the earnest of our inheritance until the redemption of the purchased possession, unto the praise of his glory.

The Church is in a Season of Profound of Change

The Angel of the Lord said that the arrival of the prophet had already taken place. As to the true infilling, I knew in my spirit he was describing more than just another Pentecostal blessing, feeling, or sensation. This baptism would not produce another man-made denomination or religious system, but a genuine change in the life of the believer. He added, "This time will be much different."

The angel of the Lord explained that the true baptism of the Holy Spirit would prepare the way for the *white eagle*. He said the white eagle represented a revelation of the fullness of Jesus Christ, not just a greater knowledge of Him but an infilling and *indwelling* of the very character and virtues of Jesus. This revelation would produce the living Word made flesh again, not just in one man as in the days of the Lord Jesus Christ but in a whole company of believers. This message would act as a plumb line, a measuring device to gauge the uprightness of all Words given to the end time bride of Jesus Christ. I spoke out to those in the room, "The world has never seen what it will see in the bride. Fools will mock and reject it, some religious leaders will scorn it, but His true bride will receive it with gladness."

I believe these words were referring to the Lord doing a new thing that will not follow historical revival patterns but will have a distinct model and administration. It will be an expansion of the ministry model of the Lord Jesus Christ as seen in the Gospels. It will be authority and power functioning and flowing in a corporate body of believers especially chosen for this purpose, even before the foundation of the world.

I then heard him say something odd, "Things are stuck on Mount Zion. The saints are stuck; they have climbed as far as they can and it seems they cannot move any higher into the virtues and attributes of Jesus." He added that I should not give in to worry.

This is referring to the old successes in the Glory. We must press into the new.

Suddenly before me was this beautiful pyramid shaped Mount Zion. It was the third time I had seen this massive mountain in vision. As I looked closer I could see the saints climbing among its cliffs, scattered along the sides of the mountain. Some had reached higher places than others, but all were moving slowly toward the top. I was getting a closer look than I ever had before and now I could see the roughness of the slopes and the rocky, jagged terrain. Small rocks tumbled off the ledges, loosened by the climbers. There were also large, unstable boulders that could become dislodged and crush the climbers in their paths. Some had climbed to places where they were unable to navigate obstacles up ahead. Some had to stop because there was no place to get a foothold or even dig in with their hands and pull themselves higher. I was blessed to see their progress but started feeling sad that more and more were becoming stalled with no way around the hindrances. It appeared that most of them would be forced to retreat and re-navigate their ascent.

The angel of the Lord startled my sad contemplation when he again reminded me, "Don't worry."

I saw a flash of movement overhead. It was the little white dove circling the top of the mountain. A fresh anointing began showering down and I knew it was being released by the presence of the dove. Suddenly I saw clearly the word "eagle" embedded in the stone face. I heard the saints begin to shout and rejoice as the fresh anointing fell on them like a blanket. They started shouting to those below, "We can make it, keep on climbing!" Someone replied, "How do you know? "Look up!" Everyone could see the dove still circling the mountain and in the distance something else was approaching. We watched as it drew closer. Someone shouted, "It's the white eagle!"

I was deeply concerned about the saints standing at the bottom of the mountain. I felt that the lateness of the hour would make it impossible for them to make it to the top. I asked aloud, "How will they ever make it to the top?"

Suddenly the white eagle came swooping down low on the side of the mountain and then up near the top again. He drew in close, nudging the saints, encouraging them to climb higher and not to give up. I heard the eagle scream out with a natural call and then suddenly he began to cry out in a powerful voice, "When you have climbed as high as you can, I will bear you on My wings to the top of Zion. My bride will make it to the top; I will give her My virtues, I'll carry her, the rest of the way. Even as I bore Israel out of Egypt on My wings, so will I carry you to the top of Mt. Zion." I joined the other saints in screaming; "Great white eagle, come and take us on your wings."

I knew in my spirit that this would in no way constitute a short cut; we would not be able to by-pass any of the lessons, preparations or impartations. This *bearing up* would only happen in the hour when we could not climb any higher on our own. It also spoke of an end to all of our human striving to be qualified as overcomers, and a new place where we would finally emerge *totally* dependent on the Lord Jesus.

I pray that we are now entering into the season of revelation that will lift us to the top of Mount Zion, and cause us to be seated with our beloved Bridegroom in His throne. We are meant to be part of this Prototype Church and the way has been laid before us. The provision, safety and encouragements are being released.

Chapter Twenty Three
The Fire of God In Power

The Church has denied the power of God. God wants to release His Fire Power. In Job 26, we find a list of vivid examples of God's power as the creator and sustainer of the universe.

Job 26:7 He stretcheth out the north over the empty place, *and* hangeth the earth upon nothing.

Job 26:11-14 The pillars of heaven tremble and are astonished at his reproof. He divideth the sea with his power, and by his understanding he smiteth through the proud. By his spirit he hath garnished the heavens; his hand hath formed the crooked serpent. Lo, these *are* parts of his ways: but how little a portion is heard of him? but the thunder of his power who can understand?

The word *thunder* here means "to cause to roar."

Job 37:1 At this also my heart trembleth, and is moved out of his place.

Exodus 19:12 And thou shalt set bounds unto the people round about, saying, Take heed to yourselves, *that ye* go *not* up into the mount, or touch the border of it: whosoever toucheth the mount shall be surely put to death:

A loud trumpet sound was the cue to assemble together.

Exodus 19:20 And the LORD came down upon mount Sinai, on the top of the mount: and the LORD called Moses *up* to the top of the mount; and Moses went up.

I guess this was one of God's ways of getting the people to take Him seriously. With precision timing, on the morning of the third day, the big action started. The Creator of the universe unleashed enough of His raw power that,

Exodus 19:16 And it came to pass on the third day in the morning, that there were thunders and lightnings, and a thick cloud upon the mount, and the voice of the trumpet exceeding loud; so that all the people that *was* in the camp trembled.

They saw and heard "thunderings and lightnings" as Mount Sinai became a raging inferno with smoke billowing everywhere. At the same time the whole mountain quaked violently and the trumpet sound became louder and louder.

Hebrews 12:18 For ye are not come unto the mount that might be touched, and that burned with fire, nor unto blackness, and darkness, and tempest,

Although Moses was well used to having fiery encounters with the great "I AM," this one scared him.

Hebrews 12:21 And so terrible was the sight, *that* Moses said, I exceedingly fear and quake:)

God spoke to Moses, calling him to visit with Him on the top of that flaming mountain, and He didn't say He would turn down the thermostat. I'd say that was the ultimate trip of a person being taken out of his comfort zone, wouldn't you? Don't ever underestimate the spiritual ambition of this man, Moses. He wanted to know God and was prepared to obey Him in doing so, even if it meant being burned to a crisp in The Fire of God the process! Don't think that's an exaggeration, because God commanded Moses—before he made the trip up the mountain—to warn the priests and the people not to attempt to get too close to Him for that very reason.

Exodus 19:24 And the LORD said unto him, Away, get thee down, and thou shalt come up, thou, and Aaron with thee: but let not the priests and the people break through to come up unto the LORD, lest he break forth upon them.

The children of Israel couldn't bear to hear the loud voice of God speaking to them directly in that setting. They opted for the voice of a man. Whereas, the Bible says Moses went toward God in the thick darkness. How desperate are we for intimate friendship with God? I would rather be close to God in the darkest circumstances of life than are with the crowd in the seeming safety of their comfort zones. The safest place at all times is under the shadow of God's wings, regardless of the temperature. And remember,

John 8:12 Then spake Jesus again unto them, saying, I am the light of the world: he that followeth me shall not walk in darkness, but shall have the light of life.

1John 1:5 This then is the message which we have heard of him, and declare unto you, that God is light, and in him is no darkness at all.

So the nearer we are to Him, the more light we'll experience. He promises us that His Word is a lamp to our feet and a light to our path.

Psalms 119:105 NUN. Thy word *is* a lamp unto my feet, and a light unto my path.

Have you ever thought about God's miraculous protection that Moses must have experienced for him to have made it through that inferno to keep his appointment with the Fire-Maker that day? Talk about the fire of God's power of protection! When God wanted to identify the supremacy of His Being to a nation, He chose to demonstrate it by fire falling from Heaven and consuming water-saturated wood.

1Kings 18:20-38 So Ahab sent unto all the children of Israel, and gathered the prophets together unto mount Carmel. And Elijah came unto all the people, and said, How long halt ye between two opinions? if the LORD *be* God, follow him: but if Baal, *then* follow him. And the people answered him not a word. Then said Elijah unto the people, I, *even* I only, remain a prophet of the LORD; but Baal's prophets *are* four hundred and fifty men. Let them therefore give us two bullocks; and let them choose one bullock for themselves, and cut it in pieces, and lay *it* on wood, and put no fire *under:* and I will dress the other bullock, and lay *it* on wood, and put no fire *under:* And call ye on the name of your gods, and I will call on the name of the LORD: and the God that answereth by fire, let him be God. And all the people answered and said, It is well spoken. And Elijah said unto the prophets of Baal, Choose you one bullock for yourselves, and dress *it* first; for ye *are* many; and call on the name of your gods, but put no fire *under*. And they took the bullock which was given them, and they dressed *it,* and called on the name of Baal from morning even until noon, saying, O Baal, hear us. But *there was* no voice, nor any that answered. And they leaped upon the altar which was made. And it came to pass at noon, that Elijah mocked them, and said, Cry aloud: for he *is* a god; either he is talking, or he is pursuing, or he is in a journey, *or* peradventure he sleepeth, and must be awaked. And they cried aloud, and cut themselves after their manner with knives and lancets, till the blood gushed out upon them. And it came to pass, when midday was past, and they prophesied until the *time* of the offering of the *evening* sacrifice, that *there was* neither voice, nor any to answer, nor any that regarded. And Elijah said unto all the people, Come near unto me. And all the people came near unto him. And he repaired the altar of the LORD *that was* broken down. And Elijah took twelve stones, according to the number of the tribes of the sons of Jacob, unto whom the word of the LORD came, saying, Israel shall be thy name: And with the stones he built an altar in the name of the LORD: and he made a trench about the altar, as great as would contain two measures of seed. And he put the wood in order, and cut the bullock in pieces, and laid *him* on the wood, and said, Fill four barrels with water, and pour *it* on the burnt sacrifice, and on the wood. And he said, Do *it* the second time. And they did *it* the second time. And he said, Do *it* the third time. And they did *it* the third time. And the water ran round about the altar; and he filled the trench also with water. And it came to pass at *the time of* the offering of the *evening* sacrifice, that Elijah the prophet came near, and said, LORD God of Abraham, Isaac, and of Israel, let it be known this day that thou *art* God in Israel, and *that* I *am* thy servant, and *that* I have done all these things at thy word. Hear me,

O LORD, hear me, that this people may know that thou *art* the LORD God, and *that* thou hast turned their heart back again. Then the fire of the LORD fell, and consumed the burnt sacrifice, and the wood, and the stones, and the dust, and licked up the water that *was* in the trench.

When God wanted to display the limitlessness of His power to show up the powerlessness of His enemies, He chose a man named Elijah to be His ambassador and spokesman who was impressed only with the might and majesty of the One who had planned the showdown (God Himself). The winner of the contest on Mount Carmel was to be proven by the truth of the challenge, "The God who answers by fire, He is God."

Deuteronomy 4:24 For the LORD thy God *is* a consuming fire, *even* a jealous God.

Hebrews 12:29 For our God *is* a consuming fire.

So, all He has to do is show up and choose to put that part of Himself on display. To the opposing party, it's hardly a contest. The outcome is determined before the show starts.

1Kings 18:26 And they took the bullock which was given them, and they dressed *it,* and called on the name of Baal from morning even until noon, saying, O Baal, hear us. But *there was* no voice, nor any that answered. And they leaped upon the altar which was made.

1Kings 18:28 And they cried aloud, and cut themselves after their manner with knives and lancets, till the blood gushed out upon them.

Then they spent all afternoon supposedly prophesying that the action would surely come. Now, that's a description of the determination and despair that comes from total disillusionment. That's when God loves to take center stage. He answered a brief, two-sentence prayer from His fearless prophet,

1Kings 18:38 Then the fire of the LORD fell, and consumed the burnt sacrifice, and the wood, and the stones, and the dust, and licked up the water that *was* in the trench.

We all know that water is used to quench fire, but when the fire of God's power is unleashed, the reverse takes place and the fire consumes the water. Now that's God power! How embarrassing a defeat for the opposition, and what a victory for the undefeated champion, God Almighty!

Then Elijah finished the showdown by executing the 450 prophets of Baal plus 400 prophets of Asherah.

Psalms 104:32 He looketh on the earth, and it trembleth: he toucheth the hills, and they smoke.

Now listen to the prophet Micah as he describes what it's like when God flexes His muscles.

Micah 1:3, 4 For, behold, the LORD cometh forth out of his place, and will come down, and tread upon the high places of the earth. And the mountains shall be molten under him, and the valleys shall be cleft, as wax before the fire, *and* as the waters *that are* poured down a steep place.

Think about that for raw power. Perhaps one of the reasons why unbelief is so rampant in those who profess to be followers of the Lord Jesus is because they have never taken the time to study the biblical descriptions of God's awesome power in action, in whichever form it may be manifest.

The prophet Nahum announced to the people of Nineveh, a hundred years after God had demonstrated His mercy by sparing it from judgment.

Nahum 1:3 The LORD *is* slow to anger, and great in power, and will not at all acquit *the wicked:* the LORD hath his way in the whirlwind and in the storm, and the clouds *are* the dust of his feet.

The Assyrians had forgotten their previous revival and true spiritual awakening and had turned back to their former sins of violence and idolatry. Nahum proclaims to them the downfall of the same city as he describes how God's power will be manifest:

Nahum 1:5, 6 The mountains quake at him, and the hills melt, and the earth is burned at his presence, yea, the world, and all that dwell therein. Who can stand before his indignation? and who can abide in the fierceness of his anger? his fury is poured out like fire, and the rocks are thrown down by him.

This is a description of mountains moving, shaking, and melting at God's presence, while the whole planet is traumatized. That means He doesn't have to do anything but show up and the most awesome displays of the fire of God's power are activated. God calls us to tremble before Him as we pause to consider His creative power in doing the absolutely impossible-to-man things at times of their desperate need.

Psalms 114:7, 8 Tremble, thou earth, at the presence of the Lord, at the presence of the God of Jacob; Which turned the rock *into* a standing water, the flint into a fountain of waters.

The impossible-to-man doesn't impress, intimidate, faze, or challenge God. The fire of God's power and purposes in the affairs of mankind can't be stopped. At the same time God calls us to tremble at His presence, in the fear of the Lord, as we ponder His awesome control over the elements He created.

Jeremiah 5:22 Fear ye not me? saith the LORD: will ye not tremble at my presence, which have placed the sand *for* the bound of the sea by a perpetual decree, that it cannot pass it: and though the waves thereof toss themselves, yet can they not prevail; though they roar, yet can they not pass over it?

Psalms 99:1 The LORD reigneth; let the people tremble: he sitteth *between* the cherubims; let the earth be moved.

Psalms 99:4 The king's strength also loveth judgment; thou dost establish equity, thou executest judgment and righteousness in Jacob.

Romans 8:1 *There is* therefore now no condemnation to them which are in Christ Jesus, who walk not after the flesh, but after the Spirit.

The Church is in a Season of Profound of Change

We mortals have become so accustomed to noise and action when we meet together that most are uncomfortable when waiting in silence before God.

The fire of God's power is manifest in many different ways. But none more effectively than when the Word of God describes the explosive effect of the gospel when presented in the power of the Holy Spirit through surrendered, clean vessels to needy souls.

Romans 1:16 For I am not ashamed of the gospel of Christ: for it is the power of God unto salvation to every one that believeth; to the Jew first, and also to the Greek.

This is the greatest power of God unto salvation.

Chapter Twenty Four
The Kingly Anointing

The Prototype Church is not going to be established without the Judgment of God starting at the house of God.

Eli's sons didn't resist temptation and Eli didn't rebuke them. His sons lay with the women who served at the doorway of the tent of meeting.

1Samuel 2:22 Now Eli was very old, and heard all that his sons did unto all Israel; and how they lay with the women that assembled *at* the door of the tabernacle of the congregation.

1Samuel 3:13 For I have told him that I will judge his house for ever for the iniquity which he knoweth; because his sons made themselves vile, and he restrained them not.

God knew and He was going to do something! The Father will not be mocked and He has a standard of righteousness, a divine evaluation or plumb-line.

Galatians 6:7 Be not deceived; God is not mocked: for whatsoever a man soweth, that shall he also reap.

Today many preachers and ministries are being examined by God because it's judgment time concerning the house of God. How many ministers and preachers are going to be in trouble soon because they wouldn't confront some of the controversial issues in their churches and ministries? Their attitude is: It's good enough! Come on, we don't want to rock the boat. We want to be politically correct and draw in as many people as possible. Just think about how much money they give. We don't want to speak into that situation or become confrontational. We don't want to be a prophetic voice.

I've ministered in Churches where the Leadership freaks out when I begin to preach against sin. When God releases His judgment in the Church it usually affects the Leaders first.

So often what we say and do in church all looks good and it all sounds good, but it's full of compromise. We need to have a message today of conviction that leads to repentance; a message that calls sin for what it is. Yes, we need to walk in love and in wisdom, but if there's something going on in our ministries or churches, if there's something going on in the lives of those that God has put in our care, we have a responsibility to speak up. Then it's off our hands.

Eli's attitude was, Oh, I don't want to do anything about that. We don't want to be like him, doing nothing about immorality, worldliness or prayerlessness. Prayerlessness, apathy and love without passion-all needs to be addressed. So God came to Eli and judged his house. The apostle Peter spoke about God's judgment coming first to the household of God:

1Peter 4:17 For the time *is come* that judgment must begin at the house of God: and if *it* first *begin* at us, what shall the end *be* of them that obey not the gospel of God?

God removed the priestly mantle from Eli and his household: Eli, you're not going to be in the house anymore. I'm about to raise up a faithful priest. I want a man who's going to do what's in My heart and a man that's going to do what's in My mind. Young Samuel was the one God chose and raised up because He saw this young boy's faithful heart and He knew Samuel would do His will. Samuel became God's trusted prophet, one who grieved over sin and one who had the authority to anoint David as King.

1Samuel 16:1 And the LORD said unto Samuel, How long wilt thou mourn for Saul, seeing I have rejected him from reigning over Israel? fill thine horn with oil, and go, I will send thee to Jesse the Bethlehemite: for I have provided me a king among his sons.

1Samuel 3:19 And Samuel grew, and the LORD was with him, and did let none of his words fall to the ground.

Samuel spoke prophetic wisdom because he knew God's heart. We can't move into the kingly anointing without the prophetic anointing, and we can't move into the prophetic anointing without the priestly anointing. Also we shouldn't forget that even though David had a devoted heart toward the Lord, he was involved in a great sin when he lived in Jerusalem. But his heart was different than Eli's because he repented when Nathan the prophet came to him about what he had done. Eli never repented. And because David repented, God wasn't forced to remove his kingly anointing, but he did suffer God ordained consequences because of what he did.

2Samuel 12:10, 11 Now therefore the sword shall never depart from thine house; because thou hast despised me, and hast taken the wife of Uriah the Hittite to be thy wife. Thus saith the LORD, Behold, I will raise up evil against thee out of thine own house, and I will take thy wives before thine eyes, and give *them* unto thy neighbour, and he shall lie with thy wives in the sight of this sun.

As I said earlier, God will not be mocked. Christians are accountable for their actions, and Christian leaders even more so, because they have influence with people from all walks of life and they set a standard that people will follow.

Christians prove that they have the heart of a faithful priest when they esteem the holiness of God and when they're only concerned with doing God's will. Then they'll have what it takes to carry the kingly anointing. But what is the kingly anointing? The kingly anointing involves a wide scope of spiritual authority because it releases a corporate anointing.

Here's an example of what this means. The kingly anointing is in operation when we see one thousand demon possessed people coming to the altar and when we pray in the name of Jesus, one thousand people go through mass deliverance. Ministering in a crusade setting is a different dimension than praying for someone in a counseling room setting, one on one. There is an anointing for the counseling setting and that's good, but there's an anointing called the kingly anointing that God wants to impart so that the masses are touched simultaneously. For instance there might be tens of thousands of people at one of our crusades and in Jesus name I'll command the blind to see. Then I'll command the deaf to hear. And many, simultaneously, will see and hear instantly! When this happens, it's the corporate anointing. We need more of this! I believe God wants to release a whole new focus and new level of authority in the body of Christ to advance His kingdom.

I see this new level in our ministry here at Revival Waves of Glory. We're being led to pray for thousands at one time in our crusades, commanding different diseases to leave. And many people are healed and delivered all at once! I don't have four hours to cast out a devil. There has to be a level of authority and power in the church where we can see a whole stadium healed at one time! We need this level of anointing! In the future we might have thousands of people who are crippled at our crusades. We won't be able to lay hands on them all individually. When masses of people are healed and delivered, then the kingly anointing is demonstrating God's power and this will transform cities, regions and nations.

I believe there is an increase in the level of anointing and authority that is coming upon leaders and ministries to bring breakthroughs in cities, regions and nations! This is the Prototype Church coming in its fullness.

Some leaders and ministries will affect cities because their present level of authority is for cities. Others will affect regions and others will affect nations. There are different levels of authority. We need to prepare our hearts to receive a whole lot more from God!

In order for God to strongly support us, we must be radically sold out to him like King David and Samuel. And so I want to ask a few questions and invite us to take some time before the Lord examining our hearts.

How do we take care of the lamp stand? Scripture says: Aaron shall burn on it sweet incense every morning; when he tends the lamps, he shall burn incense on it.

Exodus 30:7, 8 And Aaron shall burn thereon sweet incense every morning: when he dresseth the lamps, he shall burn incense upon it. And when Aaron lighteth the lamps at even, he shall burn incense upon it, a perpetual incense before the LORD throughout your generations.

Prayer was going on simultaneously while Aaron was tending the lamp. Prayer makes the ground of our heart fertile so that we can begin to hear and receive revelation. When it's all said and done, what does our week look like?

I felt the Lord say that He wants to bring us into a whole new level of intimacy, through soaking and seeking, because that's how we're going to go deeper. So let's take time to be with the Lord and not book our week up so there's no room for God in our lives. Are we walking in humility and devotion to the Lord? If so, then we're in a safe place spiritually and when the Lion roars and pronounces judgment against our enemies we won't be swept into it. Rather, we'll see bondages break and freedom come to our sons and daughters. Do we sense our hearts have become a little callused and cold? Let's be like Samuel and minister to the Lord and ask Him to renew our passion for Him. If you want to come back and buy gold refined in the fire, I want you to do that today.

Revelations 3:14-22 And unto the angel of the church of the Laodiceans write; These things saith the Amen, the faithful and true witness, the beginning of the creation of God; I know thy works, that thou art neither cold nor hot: I would thou wert cold or hot. So then because thou art lukewarm, and neither cold nor hot, I will spue thee out of my mouth. Because thou sayest, I am rich, and increased with goods, and have need of nothing; and knowest not that thou art wretched, and miserable, and poor, and blind, and naked: I counsel thee to buy of me gold tried in the fire, that thou mayest be rich; and white raiment, that thou mayest be clothed, and *that* the shame of thy nakedness do not appear; and anoint thine eyes with

The Church is in a Season of Profound of Change

eyesalve, that thou mayest see. As many as I love, I rebuke and chasten: be zealous therefore, and repent. Behold, I stand at the door, and knock: if any man hear my voice, and open the door, I will come in to him, and will sup with him, and he with me. To him that overcometh will I grant to sit with me in my throne, even as I also overcame, and am set down with my Father in his throne. He that hath an ear, let him hear what the Spirit saith unto the churches.

Your relationship with God might need to be made right. God may be challenging you to begin to confront an issue.

Chapter Twenty Five
The Kingdom Mandate

This is the best time for God's Presence and power that is being released. In this hour, the Kingdom of Heaven is advancing in the earth at an incredible rate. We are beginning to witness the coming forth of past seed sown in humanity—both good and evil. The intercessory prayers made by the saints over the last thousand years will release a shockwave of the Glory of God in the earth never witnessed in the history of humankind.

As this happens, we will see a massive Kingdom shift that will result in the harvest coming with alarming demonstrations of supernatural signs, wonders, miracles, healing, and deliverance. This is when we really embrace what God is saying.

The Body of Christ is coming into a unity in the Spirit that will grow into a maturity in the full knowledge of Jesus, arriving at the complete and total measure and stature of the fullness in Christ.

Ephesians 4:13 Till we all come in the unity of the faith, and of the knowledge of the Son of God, unto a perfect man, unto the measure of the stature of the fulness of Christ:

In order for this to happen, we must know the power of the Gospel we preach and what our mandate is.

There have been many attributes and truths about the Kingdom that have been preached throughout the ages, with a great deal of success manifesting certain Kingdom realities in power. Each of these truths is essential for establishing the Kingdom on the earth. Even today there are many truths being preached: salvation, deliverance, healing, miracles, and so forth. These are wonderful within themselves, but they alone are not the Gospel of the Kingdom of God It's important for us to understand that Jesus did not come preaching salvation, nor did He preach miracles, deliverance, or healing. Jesus came preaching the Gospel of the Kingdom, and as He did, He manifested deliverance, healing, signs, and wonders. The majority of His parables were about the Kingdom of God. As a matter of fact, Jesus mentions or talks about the Kingdom of Heaven or the Kingdom of God one hundred twenty nine times in the four Gospels alone, making it His most talked-about subject.

Even after His resurrection, Jesus appeared to His disciples and immediately began to talk with them about the subject that was foremost on His mind—the Kingdom.

Acts 1:3 To whom also he shewed himself alive after his passion by many infallible proofs, being seen of them forty days, and speaking of the things pertaining to the kingdom of God:

Jesus was saying to His disciples, "Now that everything is set back in order, let's get on with the family business of pushing back darkness and establishing the dominion of the Kingdom of God on earth.

Luke 4:43 And he said unto them, I must preach the kingdom of God to other cities also: for therefore am I sent.

What a powerful statement! Jesus said His earthly mission was to preach the good news of the Kingdom—this was one of the chief purposes for being sent from the Father. Jesus brought salvation, healing, The Kingdom Mandate and deliverance. He performed miracles, signs, and wonders and did it all while preaching the Gospel of the Kingdom of God. When the Kingdom is preached, there should *always* be a demonstration of power.

We must preach the Gospel not the watered down version of today's religious Church.

Building a Prototype Church

1Corinthians 4:20 For the kingdom of God *is* not in word, but in power.

Signs, wonders, miracles, and healings always follow the preaching of the *genuine* Gospel of the Kingdom.

Mark 16:15 And he said unto them, Go ye into all the world, and preach the gospel to every creature.

This being said, it is critical that we know and understand what Gospel we are to preach. We've already established that Jesus, from start to finish of His earthly ministry, preached, prayed, and performed the Gospel of the Kingdom. But what about others in the New Testament; what Gospel did they preach?

Luke 9:1, 2 Then he called his twelve disciples together, and gave them power and authority over all devils, and to cure diseases. And he sent them to preach the kingdom of God, and to heal the sick.

He then sent them out as apostles, commissioning them to preach the Kingdom of God.

Luke 10:9 And heal the sick that are therein, and say unto them, The kingdom of God is come nigh unto you.

Acts 19:8 And he went into the synagogue, and spake boldly for the space of three months, disputing and persuading the things concerning the kingdom of God.

Acts 28:23 And when they had appointed him a day, there came many to him into *his* lodging; to whom he expounded and testified the kingdom of God, persuading them concerning Jesus, both out of the law of Moses, and *out of* the prophets, from morning till evening.

Acts 28:31 Preaching the kingdom of God, and teaching those things which concern the Lord Jesus Christ, with all confidence, no man forbidding him.

Others preached the Gospel of the Kingdom, like Philip, causing many men and women to be baptized.

The Church is in a Season of Profound of Change

Acts 8:12 But when they believed Philip preaching the things concerning the kingdom of God, and the name of Jesus Christ, they were baptized, both men and women.

Matthews 24:24 For there shall arise false Christs, and false prophets, and shall shew great signs and wonders; insomuch that, if *it were* possible, they shall deceive the very elect.

Clearly, the Gospel that we are called to preach, demonstrate, and live is the Gospel of the Kingdom.

Matthew 6:10 Thy kingdom come. Thy will be done in earth, as *it is* in heaven.

From the verse above, Jesus made it very clear how to know His perfect will; we can conclude that God's will is *His Kingdom being birthed on the earth*. What, then, is God's Kingdom? We can break down the word *kingdom* into two words: *king's domain.* The Kingdom of God is the area in which His dominion is established—it's the rule and reign of King Jesus. God's intent is that His will be done on earth just like it is being done in Heaven—that the physical domain of earth would resemble the spiritual domain of Heaven, as an extension or a territory of the Kingdom of God in Heaven. Another definition for the word *domain* is "a territory over which dominion is exercised; complete and absolute ownership of land." It is a king's territory.

God gave us the mandate to rule Earth and subdue, maintain, and transform the planet, with its regions and inhabitants, into a Kingdom territory patterned to look like the Kingdom of Heaven. Our mission is to make this place (earth) look like that place (Heaven). His original plan was to extend His heavenly domain on the earth through a family of sons and daughters—not servants. Servants have no authority and are not part of the Father's house, but serve as subjects in the master's quarters.

Galatians 4:1-7 Now I say, *That* the heir, as long as he is a child, differeth nothing from a servant, though he be lord of all; But is under tutors and governors until the time appointed of the father. Even so we, when we were children, were in bondage under the elements of the world: But when the fulness of the time was come, God sent forth his Son, made of a woman, made under the law, To redeem them that were under the law, that we might receive the adoption of sons. And because ye are sons, God hath sent forth the Spirit of his Son into your hearts, crying, Abba, Father. Wherefore thou art no more a servant, but a son; and if a son, then an heir of God through Christ.

Sons and daughters, however, have ownership and a legal right in the house to come and go as they choose and to share in all family provision and decisions. We are the Family of God. The Father's plan was that we would share His rulership as a family of sons and daughters who would rule the earth on His behalf.

The first commandment God gave humankind was to subdue the earth and have dominion.

Genesis 1:26-30 And God said, Let us make man in our image, after our likeness: and let them have dominion over the fish of the sea, and over the fowl of the air, and over the cattle, and over all the earth, and over every creeping thing that creepeth upon the earth. So God created man in his *own* image, in the image of God created he him; male and female created he them. And God blessed them, and God said unto them, Be fruitful, and multiply, and replenish the earth, and subdue it: and have dominion over the fish of the sea, and over the fowl of the air, and over every living thing that moveth upon the earth. And God said, Behold, I have given you every herb bearing seed, which *is* upon the face of all the earth, and every tree, in the which *is* the fruit of a tree yielding seed; to you it shall be for meat. And to every beast of the earth, and to every fowl of the air, and to every thing that creepeth upon the earth, wherein *there is* life, *I have given* every green herb for meat: and it was so.

Adam and Eve's job was to extend the boundaries of the Garden to the ends of the earth Through Jesus' death and resurrection, He took back the keys of the Kingdom, the authority and rightful dominion of earth, and gave them back to humankind for another shot, born-again children of God around the world have the privilege and capacity to co-labor with Christ to establish and advance His Kingdom in the earth *Co-laboring* with Christ is humans working with God. The Spirit of God lives in us; we are His hands and feet. We are the Body of Christ on the earth today, able to do the works Jesus did—and even greater works.

John 14:12 Verily, verily, I say unto you, He that believeth on me, the works that I do shall he do also; and greater *works* than these shall he do; because I go unto my Father.

We know that Christianity was never intended to be about religion, but relationship. However, there is a legal aspect to true Christianity. Many in the western world don't have a clue about Kingdom operations. Our countries are not monarchies run by a supreme royal authority, but self-governed democracies which originated from the Greek and Roman governments. In a monarchy, the king and queen have supreme authority over all the land, territory, and people within their kingdom. Everyone within the kingdom looks upon them with utmost respect and honor. They hold all rule and authority—having but to speak the *word* and it will be done. The sons and daughters in the royal bloodline carry that same authority because they are part of the royal family. We too are citizens of a heavenly Kingdom; a Kingdom not of this world.

Philippians 3:20 For our conversation is in heaven; from whence also we look for the Saviour, the Lord Jesus Christ:

John 18:36 Jesus answered, My kingdom is not of this world: if my kingdom were of this world, then would my servants fight, that I should not be delivered to the Jews: but now is my kingdom not from hence.

Because we are citizens of Heaven, we have a legal right to access all the blessings of Heaven. We know that there is no sickness in Heaven, no disease, no poverty, no depression, no sin, and no broken families. Therefore, we have authorized permission to not only *access* healing, wholeness, prosperity, deliverance, and restoration, but to take those things and *manifest them on Earth.* We are a legal people who have the right of full government and power to rule and regulate planet earth. We are the offspring of

God; we have our Father's royal blood and DNA flowing through our spirits. Jesus is the King of many kings and Lord of many lords.

Revelations 19:16 And he hath on *his* vesture and on his thigh a name written, KING OF KINGS, AND LORD OF LORDS.

1Timothy 6:15 Which in his times he shall shew, *who is* the blessed and only Potentate, the King of kings, and Lord of lords;

We are the kings and lords over earth. We are *landlords* so to speak. Heaven is God's territory and earth is humanity's territory. God designed us for the rule of earth, not the rule of Heaven. This also is why we'll return to rule and reign on a new earth.

Psalms 115:15, 16 Ye *are* blessed of the LORD which made heaven and earth. The heaven, *even* the heavens, *are* the LORD'S: but the earth hath he given to the children of men.

CHAPTER TWENTY SIX
Spiritual Dynamics

We are to see the dynamics of God's Kingdom unfold in the greatest outpouring of God's Spirit.

Matthew 4:17 From that time Jesus began to preach, and to say, Repent: for the kingdom of heaven is at hand.

That message was not only for individuals in and through whom the Kingdom was to be established, but also for the Church, the entire body of believers It was a call to turn from our old way of thinking and embrace Kingdom thinking because the Kingdom of God is *now*. The act of repentance is changing our way of thinking from the natural to the spiritual. It is discarding, turning from, and abandoning former thought patterns and processes and adopting the Source of all truth—Jesus Christ.

True repentance is receiving the mind of Christ and aligning ourselves (spirit, soul, and body) with the Kingdom of Heaven. The Kingdom of God is always present tense—it is *now*.

It is time now to change your way of thinking from the old way to the new way, which is the Kingdom way.

Jesus told Nicodemus, a ruler of the Jews, that to *see* the Kingdom of God in operation we must be born from above. What does that mean and what is its significance to us?

John 3:1-8 There was a man of the Pharisees, named Nicodemus, a ruler of the Jews: The same came to Jesus by night, and said unto him, Rabbi, we know that thou art a teacher come from God: for no man can do these miracles that thou doest, except God be with him. Jesus answered and said unto him, Verily, verily, I say unto thee, Except a man be born again, he cannot see the kingdom of God. Nicodemus saith unto him, How can a man be born when he is old? can he enter the second time into his mother's womb, and be born? Jesus answered, Verily, verily, I say unto thee, Except a man be born of water and *of* the Spirit, he cannot enter into the kingdom of God. That which is born of the flesh is flesh; and that which is born of the Spirit is spirit. Marvel not that I said unto thee, Ye must be born again. The wind bloweth where it listeth, and thou hearest the sound thereof, but canst not tell whence it cometh, and whither it goeth: so is every one that is born of the Spirit.

Jesus told Nicodemus that in order to *see* the Kingdom of God in operation, he must be born from above. He was saying to Nicodemus that he could never see the Kingdom, nor experience it, unless he was first born from another dimension—a higher dimension. We could also say that we must be "borne" or lifted from above. We must be airborne—lifted from the natural ways of thinking and understanding—into a higher reality. We must depart from earthbound ways, with the intention of being airborne in the heavens.

An airplane, as it sits motionless, is bound by the law of gravity, but as it propels down the runway it is lifted into the air. There is another law that comes into play. The law of gravity is bent, because the law of aerodynamics takes over. So it is with the Kingdom of God. The lower laws are no longer in effect or related because *lift* begins to occur. We are subject to higher laws—the laws of spiritual aerodynamics. The Kingdom mindset is superior to the natural mindset. In the verse above, we see that those born of the flesh are born from the natural realm and are *subject to natural laws*. However, those born of the Spirit are spirit and are *no longer* subject to the natural. We can only release Kingdom currency when Kingdom thoughts are thought and Kingdom language is spoken.

The essence of repentance has very little to do with feeling sorry for something bad we've done, but rather turning from our old earthly way of thinking to a new heavenly way of being. Remember, what we meditate on and think about manifests in our lives.

Proverbs 23:7 For as he thinketh in his heart, so *is* he: Eat and drink, saith he to thee; but his heart *is* not with thee.

We are conformed to the image of what we gaze upon; this is why we are encouraged to fix our eyes on King Jesus.

Hebrews 12:2 Looking unto Jesus the author and finisher of *our* faith; who for the joy that was set before him endured the cross, despising the shame, and is set down at the right hand of the throne of God.

Matthew 6:33 But seek ye first the kingdom of God, and his righteousness; and all these things shall be added unto you.

Colossians 3:1, 2 If ye then be risen with Christ, seek those things which are above, where Christ sitteth on the right hand of God. Set your affection on things above, not on things on the earth.

We are given a command to *keep seeking* heavenly things—to purposely fix our minds and hearts on things above where Christ is seated and where we are *presently* seated with Christ.

Ephesians 2:6 And hath raised *us* up together, and made *us* sit together in heavenly *places* in Christ Jesus:

Gaining God's perspective is one of the keys that will bring about the last-day harvest. When we see the world around us with the eyes of Christ, we have tapped into the realm of *all things are possible.*

We can describe the plan of God as simple It is to extend the rule of His unseen Kingdom or spirit world into the seen Kingdom or the physical world through a family of legal heirs—sons and daughters. These offspring would act as God, on behalf of God, being His legal representatives and judiciaries on the planet, carrying out His orders and implementing His will with full governmental authority given them by their Father and older heavenly Brother, Jesus

John 20:17 Jesus saith unto her, Touch me not; for I am not yet ascended to my Father: but go to my brethren, and say unto them, I ascend unto my Father, and your Father; and *to* my God, and your God.

Romans 8:29 For whom he did foreknow, he also did predestinate *to be* conformed to the image of his Son, that he might be the firstborn among many brethren.

The only begotten Son of the Father is the prototype for the brothers and sisters, who find their way to the Father in relationship with Him and who, with Him, become the heirs of the coming Kingdom.

John 1:12 But as many as received him, to them gave he power to become the sons of God, *even* to them that believe on his name:

He gave those who believe in His name the right, ability, and privilege to become children of God. We are in a place and time where we are starting to see the children of the Kingdom come into maturity. These *seeds* are coming of age and are visibly beginning to bring forth fruit that resembles the fruit of the original *Seed*. Through His offspring, God is manifesting and establishing His Kingdom and His will on earth.

He rules the seen world from the unseen world through our spirits, and He births His initiatives through us in the physical realm. The fruitful journey of Jesus was well documented as He traveled about cities and villages, teaching in their synagogues, proclaiming the good news, the Gospel of the Kingdom of God. He cured *every* sickness, disease, and infirmity that He encountered, further preparing the soil and sowing afresh the precious seed.

Matthew 4:23 And Jesus went about all Galilee, teaching in their synagogues, and preaching the gospel of the kingdom, and healing all manner of sickness and all manner of disease among the people.

Matthew 9:35 And Jesus went about all the cities and villages, teaching in their synagogues, and preaching the gospel of the kingdom, and healing every sickness and every disease among the people.

Everywhere that He preached the gospel, Jesus manifested His power with miracles, signs, and wonders. God expects His offspring, His family, His seed, to do the same works—acting the same way as Jesus did. *Because you are sons, God has sent forth the Spirit of His Son into our hearts, crying, "Abba! Father!"*

Galatians 4:6, 7 And because ye are sons, God hath sent forth the Spirit of his Son into your hearts, crying, Abba, Father. Wherefore thou art no more a servant, but a son; and if a son, then an heir of God through Christ.

Adam's rebellion toward God ended in spiritual death, resulting in him being cut off from access to unhindered supernatural ability and the Glory of God. Adam was left to find his own way in life, filtering the world around him through his five natural senses.

It is now being discovered again in this age and time and understood afresh by a family of sons and daughters of God all around the world. All things have been put in subjection under the feet of Christ. We are the Body of Christ—so all things have been put under our feet.

There is much more but we are going to stop here. God will guide you in all you do in Building a Prototype Church.

If you enjoyed this book, you will love Volume two Transitioning Into a Prototype Church.

About the Author

Bill Vincent is no stranger to understanding the power of God. Not only has he spent over twenty years as a Minister with a strong prophetic anointing, he is now also an Apostle and Author with Revival Waves of Glory Ministries in Litchfield, IL. Along with his wife, Tabitha, he, leads a team providing apostolic oversight in all aspects of ministry, including service, personal ministry and Godly character.

Bill offers a wide range of writings and teachings from deliverance, to experiencing presence of God and developing Apostolic cutting edge Church structure. Drawing on the power of the Holy Spirit through years of experience in Revival, Spiritual Sensitivity, and deliverance ministry, Bill now focuses mainly on pursuing the Presence of God and breaking the power of the devil off of people's lives.

His books 48 and counting has since helped many people to overcome the spirits and curses of Satan. For more information or to keep up with Bill's latest releases, please visit www.revivalwavesofgloryministries.com. To contact Bill, feel free to follow him on twitter @revivalwaves.

The Church is in a Season of Profound of Change

Recommended Books

By Bill Vincent

Overcoming Obstacles

Glory: Pursuing God's Presence

Defeating the Demonic Realm

Increasing Your Prophetic Gift

Increase Your Anointing

Keys to Receiving Your Miracle

The Supernatural Realm

Waves of Revival

Increase of Revelation and Restoration

The Resurrection Power of God

Discerning Your Call of God

Apostolic Breakthrough

Glory: Increasing God's Presence

Love is Waiting – Don't Let Love Pass You By

Building a Prototype Church

The Healing Power of God

Glory: Expanding God's Presence

Receiving Personal Prophecy

Signs and Wonders

Signs and Wonders Revelations

Children Stories

The Rapture

The Secret Place of God's Power

Building a Prototype Church

Breakthrough of Spiritual Strongholds

Glory: Revival Presence of God

Overcoming the Power of Lust

Glory: Kingdom Presence of God

Transitioning to the Prototype Church

The Stronghold of Jezebel

Healing After Divorce

A Closer Relationship With God

Cover Up and Save Yourself

Desperate for God's Presence

The War for Spiritual Battles

The Church is in a Season of Profound of Change

Spiritual Leadership

Global Warning

Millions of Churches

Destroying the Jezebel Spirit

Awakening of Miracles

Deception and Consequences Revealed

Are You a Follower of Christ

Don't Let the Enemy Steal from You!

A Godly Shaking

The Unsearchable Riches of Christ

Heaven's Court System

Satan's Open Doors

Armed for Battle

The Wrestler

Spiritual Warfare: Complete Collection

Growing In the Prophetic

Faith

The Angry Fighter's Story

Understanding Heaven's Court System

Web Site:

www.revivalwavesofgloryministries.com

Most books are in multiple formats such as Hardcover, Soft-Cover, Ebook (such as Kindle & Nook), and Audio Books.

The Church is in a Season of Profound of Change

www.ingramcontent.com/pod-product-compliance
Lightning Source LLC
Chambersburg PA
CBHW052026070526
44584CB00016B/1917